W9-CLG-456

Rain Forests of the World

Volume 8
Orchid–Red Panda

MARSHALL CAVENDISH
NEW YORK • LONDON • TORONTO • SYDNEY

Marshall Cavendish Corporation
99 White Plains Road
Tarrytown, New York
10591-9001

Website: www.marshallcavendish.com

Consulting Editors: Rolf E. Johnson, Nathan E. Kraucunas

Contributing Authors: Theresa Greenaway, Jill Bailey, Michael Chinery, Malcolm Penny, Mike Linley, Philip Steele, Chris Oxlade, Ken Preston-Mafham, Rod Preston-Mafham, Clare Oliver, Don Birchfield

Discovery Books
Managing Editor: Paul Humphrey
Project Editor: Gianna Williams
Text Editor: Valerie Weber
Designer: Ian Winton
Cartographer: Stefan Chabluk
Illustrators: Jim Channell, Stuart Lafford, Christian Webb

Marshall Cavendish
Editor: Marian Armstrong
Editorial Director: Paul Bernabeo

(cover) Slender Loris

Editor's Note: Many systems of dating have been used by different cultures throughout history. *Rain Forests of the World* uses B.C.E. (Before Common Era) and C.E. (Common Era) instead of B.C. (Before Christ) and A.D. (Anno Domini, "In the Year of Our Lord") out of respect for the diversity of the world's peoples.

The publishers would like to thank the following for their permission to reproduce photographs:
424 Jurgen Sohns/Frank Lane Picture Agency, 425 Michael Fogden/Oxford Scientific Films, 426 Nick Gordon/OSF, 427 Terry Whittaker/FLPA, 428 Edward Parker/OSF, 429 Gerald S. Cubitt/Bruce Coleman, 430 Ken Preston-Mafham/Premaphotos Wildlife, 431 Nick Gordon/OSF, 432 Stan Osolinski/OSF, 433 Staffan Widstrand/Bruce Coleman, 434 Terry Whittaker/FLPA, 435 John Miles/Panos Pictures, 436 Nick Robinson/Panos Pictures, 437 Daniel Heuclin/Natural History Photographic Agency, 438 Nick Gordon/OSF, 439 & 440 Alfredo Cedeno/Panos Pictures, 441 Michael Pitts/OSF, 442 Chris Stowers/Panos Pictures, 444 Life Science Images/FLPA, 445 Rod Williams/Bruce Coleman, 446 F. Hartmann/FLPA, 447 Hans Reinhard/Bruce Coleman, 448 Luiz Claudio Marigo/Bruce Coleman, 449 G. I. Bernard/NHPA, 450 Deni Bown/OSF, 451 Luiz Claudio Marigo/Bruce Coleman, 452 Ken Preston-Mafham/Premaphotos Wildlife, 453 Richard Packwood/OSF, 454 Harold Taylor/OSF, 455 K. Ghani/NHPA, 456 Roger Tidman/FLPA, 457 Terry Whittaker/FLPA, 458 & 459 Nick Gordon/OSF, 461 Ken Preston-Mafham/Premaphotos Wildlife, 462 Stephen Dalton/NHPA, 463 Harold Taylor/OSF, 464 Sara Leigh Lewis/Panos Pictures, 465 Daniel Heuclin/NHPA, 466 Konrad Wothe/OSF, 467 A. N. T./NHPA, 468 David Haring/OSF, 469 Staffan Widstrand/Bruce Coleman, 470 Discovery Photo Library, 471 David M. Dennis/OSF, 472 Corbis, 473 Alain Compost/Bruce Coleman, 475 Zig Leszczynski/OSF, 476 John Shaw/Bruce Coleman, 477 Foto Natura Stock/FLPA, 478 Ken Preston-Mafham/Premaphotos Wildlife, 479 Ken Preston-Mafham/Premaphotos Wildlife, 480 Alain Compost/Bruce Coleman, 481 Fritz Polking/FLPA

Library of Congress Cataloging-in-Publication Data
Rain forests of the world.
v. cm.
Includes bibliographical references and index.
Contents: v. 1. Africa-bioluminescence—v. 2. Biomass-clear-cutting — v. 3. Climate and weather-emergent — v. 4. Endangered species-food web — v. 5. Forest fire-iguana — v. 6. Indonesia-manatee — v. 7. Mangrove forest-orangutan — v. 8. Orchid-red panda — v. 9. Reforestation-spider — v. 10. Squirrel-Yanomami people — v. 11. Index.
ISBN 0-7614-7254-1 (set)
1. Rain forests—Encyclopedias. 1. Marshall Cavendish Corporation.
QH86 .R39 2002
578.734—dc21

ISBN 0-7614-7254-1 (set)
ISBN 0-7614-7262-2 (vol. 8)

Printed and bound in Italy

07 06 05 04 03 02 6 5 4 3 2 1

Contents

Orchid

With over 20,000 known species, orchids make up one of the largest of all families of flowering plants. Most grow in tropical forests, though orchids of one kind or another are found almost all over the world. They even grow in the Arctic, where they are covered with snow for much of the year. Orchids are best known for the vibrant colors and bizarre shapes of many of their flowers.

KEY FACTS

- **The largest petal, called a lip, of many orchids looks and smells like female bees. Male bees try to mate with the petal, but all they manage to do is pollinate the orchids.**
- **Vanilla, used to flavor ice cream and other foods, comes from the seedpods of a climbing orchid that originated in tropical South and Central America. Today most vanilla is grown in Madagascar.**

Beautiful Lips

Most orchid flowers have three petals. One petal, known as the lip, is usually much larger and more colorful than the rest, and it can take on some very strange shapes. This is the part that normally attracts insects for pollination. In many orchids it resembles a woman's skirt, while in others it looks like any of various insects or other animals. Some orchids also employ strong scents to attract insects.

On many orchids the back of the lip is drawn out to form a hollow tube called a spur. Nectar collects in the spur; patterns on the flower often guide insects to it. The Christmas star orchid, which grows in the rain forests of Madagascar, has a spur about a foot (30 cm) long. When the English naturalist Charles Darwin saw it, he predicted that it must be pollinated by a moth with an equally long tongue. About 40 years later, naturalists discovered a hawkmoth with a 12-inch (30-cm) tongue.

Festooning the Trees

Rain forest orchids nearly all grow as epiphytes on the trunks and branches

Because they grow in large clusters, the flowers of this epiphytic orchid from Malaysia are especially conspicuous.

The bright red lip of this tiny epiphytic orchid is the part that attracts the pollinating insects. The whole flower is less than a quarter of an inch (6.5 mm) across.

of trees. They are often so numerous that the bark is completely hidden. Epiphytic orchids' spongy roots hang freely in the air, soaking up the rain that falls on them. Other roots surround the branches and obtain minerals from animal droppings and other debris that collects around them.

Orchid leaves are generally tough and oval or shaped like straps. Many species that grow in forests with rain falling only in certain seasons store water in cylindrical leaves or in bulblike stems. *Dendrophylax* species, which grow on some Caribbean islands, have no leaves at all; they carry out photosynthesis in their green roots.

IN FOCUS

Cloning Orchids

Some orchids have become rare because collectors have taken so many wild plants from the forests. There is now a much better way of supplying orchids for the horticultural trade. Small patches of cells from the shoot tips are put into special nutrient solutions; these grow into complete plants. The new plants are identical to the parents, so growers can guarantee that their plants will all have the right kinds of flowers.

Tiny Seeds

Orchid seeds are extremely small and are scattered by the wind. They contain no food reserves. A seed cannot germinate unless the soil or the bark crevice in which it lands contains a certain kind of fungus. The fungus penetrates the seed and provides it with food in the early stages of germination. This is the beginning of a complex partnership, known as a mycorrhiza, that continues throughout the orchid's life. The fungus provides the orchid with mineral nutrients, and the orchid repays the fungus with sugars and other foods.

Check these out:

- Epiphyte
- Evolution of the Rain Forest
- Flowering Plant
- Herb and Spice

Owl

Owls are instantly recognizable by their large, forward-facing eyes, their hooked beaks, and the powerful talons on their feet. They all feed upon other animals, seeking them out with their acute eyesight and hearing. Although most owls come out at night to hunt, some hunt during the day. Larger owls prey on other birds and small animals, while smaller owls catch lizards and insects.

KEY FACTS

- **Owls have been around for at least 60 million years.**
- **There are about 150 different species of owls. Around 40 of these species live in the world's major rain forest areas.**
- **The least pygmy owl from the Brazilian rain forest is only 5 to 6 in. (13 to 15 cm) tall.**

Two Types of Owls

Owls are divided into two families according to small differences in their bone structure. One family, which includes barn owls, has a heart-shaped face not found in the other owls. Three of these owl species live in rain forest areas of Australia and New Guinea: the sooty owl, the lesser sooty owl, and the Australian masked owl. They feed mainly on small mammals and birds.

The second family contains all the other types of owls living today, and they are well represented in the rain forest. One of the largest is the great horned owl, with a head-and-body length of up to 21 inches (53 cm). It lives in the temperate forests of North America as well as in the tropical rain forests of Central and South America, where it normally feeds on various rabbit-sized

A tropical screech owl eats a moth it has caught in the Amazon rain forest in Brazil.

mammals. At the other end of the range are the pygmy owls. Different species hunt in the tropical rain forests of most parts of the world, but the smallest is the least pygmy owl from Brazil, which reaches just 5 to 6 inches (13 to 15 cm) in length. These tiny owls feed mainly on insects.

Fishing and Hawk Owls

Unlike most other owls, fishing owls are specially adapted to catch fish; spiky scales covering the underside of each foot and sharp, curved claws help them hold on to their slippery prey. A number of species of fishing owls live in the rain forests, taking their prey from the streams and rivers that run through them. The Malaysian fishing owl, which can reach a body length of 17 inches (43 cm), hunts from dusk onward. It will sit on a dead branch or a tree stump above or near the water and swoop down to grab fish swimming near the surface. Besides fish, however, it will also catch small mammals, birds, frogs, and snakes whenever it comes across them.

Hawk owls have longer, slimmer bodies than other owls, and longer tails. The face disks around their eyes are smaller, which is why they look like hawks. Most of the rain forest species come from Australia, New Guinea, and the Indonesian islands. Perhaps the most hawklike is the rare Papuan hawk owl, whose tail is half as long as its body.

The Spectacled Owl

Spectacled owls are widespread in the dense rain forests of South and Central America. Their young have a much greater area of white feathers than the adults and were once thought to be a different species. They prey upon almost anything they can catch, including small mammals, birds, bats, insects, and even crabs from the edges of forest streams and rivers.

Check these out:

- Bird
- Nocturnal Animal

Palm Tree

Palms are generally slender trees with trunks that tend to stay the same thickness all the way up. They have no branches, and unlike most other trees, their trunks do not get thicker with age. The trunks of many palms, including oil palms, are clothed with old leaf stalks, making them look messy. Others, including the coconut palm, have fairly smooth trunks because the leaf stalks fall with the leaves.

A crown of large evergreen leaves with spiky stalks surrounds a single large bud at the top of the trunk. The leaves are usually divided into leaflets; many of them look like giant feathers. The largest ones are as long as 30 feet (10 m). Others spread out like the fingers of a giant hand.

About 3,000 palm species grow in the warmer parts of the world. Date palms and some others thrive in dry habitats, but most palms require moister conditions. Some even grow in mangrove swamps. Most rain forest palms belong to the understory and do not reach the canopy. Stilt roots, springing from near the base, often help hold the slender stems upright, especially when the palms are young. The most unusual species are the climbing palms known as rattans, whose slender stems snake through the canopy and reach lengths of more than 600 feet (180 m).

KEY FACTS

- **The large terminal bud of a palm, protected by spiky leaves, is known as the palm heart. Coconut palm hearts are good to eat, but removing them kills the trees.**
- **The talipot palm from Southeast Asia produces the world's biggest flower cluster. Up to 25 ft. (8 m) high, it can carry over 20 million flowers, which can produce about 250,000 fruits.**
- **The largest seeds in the world are those of the double coconut, a rare palm from the Seychelles in the Indian Ocean. The seed may be as long as 20 in. (50 cm).**

The trees in this West African oil palm plantation can yield more oil per acre than any other crop.

Big Flower Bunches

Most palm trees carry their flowers in large bunches, usually with the pollen-producing male flowers and the seed-producing female flowers in separate clusters. Although the individual flowers are

Most palm trees produce large numbers of fruits. The fruits of this sago palm are hanging from the plant like clusters of knotted ropes.

quite small and dull, the clusters provide abundant nectar for bees.

Some palms produce flowers throughout the year, but the talipot palm and some others come into flower only once in their lives. After spending many years storing up food, they produce enormous flower bunches and then die as soon as the fruit is ripe. Palm fruits range from the size of a currant to that of a basketball. Each usually consists of a single seed surrounded by a fleshy or fibrous coat.

Living Department Stores

Rain forest palms provide indigenous people with many important raw materials. They yield timber for building and for dugout canoes, as well as for fuel; their huge leaves are used for thatching; and many of the palms also provide essential foods. The starchy pith extracted from the trunk of the sago palm, for example, provides sago flour, which is the staple food for many people in Southeast Asia. The trees are cut when they are about 15 years old, and each one yields up to 900 pounds (410 kg) of pith. New trees sprout from the roots after the harvest.

The fruits and seeds of many palms yield valuable oils. The plumlike fruits of the West African oil palm are a major source of vegetable oil, which is used for making margarine, soap, and many other products. It can even be used to replace the fuel in diesel engines. Large areas of rain forest have been cleared in western Africa and in Southeast Asia to provide land for oil palm plantations.

Coconuts also yield large amounts of oil, and their fibrous outer coats are used to make coconut matting and tough ropes. Coconut palms probably originated in the coastal rain forests of Malaysia, but they are now cultivated on plantations throughout the Tropics.

IN FOCUS

Palms That Walk

Some young trees with stilt roots can move to new sites if they are knocked over by falling neighbors. The flattened trunk gradually curves upward, and new stilt roots sprout from the curve. The old base dies away, but the tree continues to grow on its new roots—perhaps 6 to 9 ft. (2 to 3 m) from where it was originally growing.

Check these out:

- Climber
- Food
- Plant
- Plantation
- Rattan
- Tree

Parasite

A parasite is an organism that lives in close association with another species and takes food from it without giving anything in return. The species that is attacked is called the host. Ectoparasites live on the outside of their host, and endoparasites live inside their host's body. Parasites do not usually kill their host.

KEY FACTS

- **Parasites produce large numbers of seeds or offspring, thus increasing the chance that some will find a host.**
- **Mosquitoes carry the microscopic malaria parasite, which probably kills more people every year than anything else. The mosquitoes themselves are not parasites.**
- ***Amyema* is a mistletoe from Australasia and Southeast Asia. It exists in several forms, each with a different host tree. The *Amyema* leaves mimic those of the trees on which they are growing.**

Parasites on the Outside

Ectoparasites, also called external parasites, are mostly bloodsucking insects, including fleas and lice as well as various flies. There are even a few parasitic earwigs that nibble the skin of rats and bats in the forests of Africa and Southeast Asia. Bloodsucking ticks, which are related to spiders, are also important ectoparasites in tropical areas. They attack a wide range of birds and mammals and also various reptiles. These bloodsuckers can all transmit disease-causing germs to humans and other animals.

Parasites on the Inside

Endoparasites include tapeworms and various other worms, many of which can make people seriously ill. Many endoparasites have complex life histories involving two or more different host species.

The bilharzia worm, for example, spends part of its life in a water snail. At the right time, it escapes into the water and waits until a human or other animal swims past. It then burrows through the skin and completes its life cycle

Dozens of tiny parasitic grubs have grown up inside this Peruvian caterpillar. They are now leaving and spinning their own cocoons on the outside of its dying body.

IN FOCUS: Ichneumons

Ichneumons are often called ichneumon flies, although they are actually related to wasps. Most of them grow up inside caterpillars and other young insects. The female ichneumon finds a suitable host and lays one or more eggs inside it. When the eggs hatch, the ichneumon grubs begin to eat the host. They start off with the reserves of fat and other nonessential parts, including some of the muscles, but as they get bigger they turn their attention to the vital organs. The host is eventually killed.

in that person or animal. Schistosomiasis, caused by bilharzia worms, is a common disease in African rain forests.

The worm that causes river blindness occurs in both Africa and tropical America. It spends part of its life in a blackfly. When the blackfly bites a person to suck their blood, the worm gets into the person's blood supply. The worm normally lives under the skin, but if it gets into the eyes, it can cause blindness.

Parasitic Plants

Parasitic plants steal some or all of their food from other plants. The most common rain forest parasites are the mistletoes and their relatives, which grow on branches in the canopy. Many of them have brilliant red or orange bird-pollinated flowers. These are partial parasites in that they get their water and minerals by sending suckers into the trees on which they grow, but their leaves contain chlorophyll and can make food using sunlight.

The other main group of parasitic rain forest plants are the root parasites, which produce their flowers close to the ground. They include the rafflesias with their enormous flowers. These plants have no roots, stems, or leaves; they absorb everything they need from the roots of lianas. Many mushrooms also live as parasites on trees. They absorb food with a network of fine threads that spread through the timber; they may eventually kill the trees on which they live.

Check these out:
Disease Fly Fungus Mosquito Rafflesia

The brightly-colored tubular flowers of this South American mistletoe are pollinated mainly by birds.

Parrot, Macaw, and Parakeet

Parrots and parakeets are some of the most colorful birds in tropical rain forests worldwide. A parrot has a rather short neck, large head, and often long tail feathers. It uses its hooked bill for cracking open nuts and seeds and for crushing fruits. Parrots are perching birds: their first two toes point forward and the third and fourth toes point backward, giving them a pincerlike grip on branches.

Parakeets, cockatoos, lorikeets, and macaws are all types of parrot. The smaller parrots include parakeets, which have long pointed tails, and lovebirds, which have short rounded tails. The smallest parrots of all are the pygmy parrots, which creep around tree trunks like woodpeckers, using their short stiff tails as supports. The macaws of Central and South America are large parrots with long tails and bare faces. Cockatoos, from Australia and New Guinea, are distinguished by the large crests on their heads.

Parrots are found at all levels of the forest, feeding on fruits, nuts, seeds, and sometimes nectar, pollen, and even insects. Some parrots, such as the lories and lorikeets, may fly long distances—up to 52 miles (85 km)—in search of flowering or fruiting trees. Most parrots roost and breed in tree hollows high up in the canopy, probably to avoid predators that can climb up from the forest floor.

KEY FACTS

- **A famous African gray parrot, Alex, was trained by university researchers to name 23 different objects, count up to 5, and recognize colors and shapes. He could also use words like *yes*, *no*, and *want* correctly.**
- **Macaws can live up to 80 years or more in captivity. In general the smaller the parrot species, the shorter its lifespan.**
- **In about one-third of parrot species, male and female are different colors. For example, the male eclectus parrot is bright green, while the female is red and blue.**

A salmon-crested cockatoo. The salmon-streaked feathers on its head are its crest, which it will erect when excited.

Chatterboxes

Parrots are extremely intelligent birds. Some species, especially the African gray parrot, can learn hundreds of words, solve

A flock of orange-winged Amazon parrots lick salt from a riverbank in Peru's Manú National Park.

complex puzzles, recognize different colors, and even count.

In the wild, parrots use a language of sounds that differs from one area to the next. They appear to learn these "local dialects" from their parents. Parrot language uses a wide range of sounds—chattering, squeaking, shrieking, screaming, and clicking. Strangely, parrots do not imitate the calls of other birds. In fact, they do not speak much at all if kept with other species of birds.

Flocks of parrots on the move can be extremely noisy. Even a small group of macaws flying through the canopy of a South American rain forest can be heard for miles. Sound is the best way to keep in touch in thick vegetation. It is also the quickest way to alert other parrots to sightings of fruiting trees or to warn of danger from large birds of prey.

The "Third Foot"

The parrot's large, hooked upper bill overlaps its smaller lower bill. The two bills are joined together by a special kind of hinge that allows the bird to use its upper bill like a grappling hook when climbing. Even big, heavy macaws can hang from branches by their bills. The fine tips of their bills are used for delicate preening.

Many parrots have beaks powerful enough to crack open nuts that a person would need a hammer to open. A series of ridges on the underside of the upper bill act as a file to keep the beak sharp. The beak grows throughout the bird's life to compensate for the tough diet and heavy wear. Parrots regularly gnaw on branches to keep their beaks trim. If caged parrots do not have appropriate food or something to gnaw, their upper bill may eventually curl down until it cuts into the bird's chin.

Moluccan cockatoos use their beaks to break open coconuts, and palm parakeets saw open palm nuts. The slender-billed cockatoo has a thin beak with a long point, which it uses like a stick to reach buried roots and bulbs.

IN FOCUS

Fond of a Drink

Lories and lorikeets, from Australia and the western Pacific, feed mainly on nectar and pollen. A lorikeet has a long, narrow bill for probing flowers and an amazing brush-tipped tongue. The brushlike structure at its tip expands to lap up nectar and pollen. When the bird is feeding on other foods such as fruits and seeds, this brush tip is drawn back into a protective cup.

Rainbow lorikeets are the most colorful of parrots. They are common around Australian campgrounds and even in cities.

Some species of cockatoo drill into crevices in bark to reach insect grubs.

The great-billed parrot of Indonesia has a large, bright red beak, which it uses to display to other birds in the flock. Parrots may threaten each other by lunging with an open beak. A bird wishing to signal submission will turn its head away to hide its beak.

Show-Offs

Most parrots are mainly green, but some are brightly colored. Surprisingly the brilliant colors of parrots are quite good camouflage among the bright green leaves, flowers, and flickering sunlight of the rain forest. Blocks of solid color help to break up the outline of the bird and make it unrecognizable from a distance. The rainbow lorikeet has patches of almost every bright color imaginable. The king parrot has an orange-red head, breast, and legs; bright green wings; blue rump; and black tail. Out in the open, bright colors probably help parrots stay together with other members of the flock.

Colors are also used for showing off. Parrots that live in flocks have a distinct pecking order. Displays are important in determining the pecking order of the birds, thus avoiding the need for fighting.

Parrots are sociable birds, living in pairs or larger groups, and they usually pair for life. In order to find a mate, male parrots show off to the females by strutting about, bowing, flicking and flapping their wings, and waggling their tails. Some may expand the brilliantly colored irises of their eyes, called eye blazing. Cockatoos erect the crests on their heads, which are often brightly colored. Many macaws have patches of bare skin around their eyes that blush pink when the birds are excited.

Parrots in Danger

Taken by the thousands to delight humans as pets for their attractive feathers and—as they become increasingly rare—as collectors' items, many parrot species are in danger. Rare species fetch huge sums on the collectors' black market. The loss of their forest habitat is the most serious cause of decline. Secondary forest—forest that has grown back after felling or fire—lacks the old hollow trees the parrots need for nesting.

Some species are being helped by cross-fostering: their eggs are placed in the nests of more common species, so they are reared by foster parents. In suitable habitats artificial nest sites can improve breeding success.

Check these out:

● **Africa** ● **Bird** ● **Endangered Species** ● **Extinction** ● **Poaching**

People of the Rain Forest

In the not too distant past, many native peoples made their home in the rain forest; most lived in harmony with their surroundings. Today just a tiny handful of these people remain in each of the main rain forest systems. As a result of the way in which Western civilizations have intruded into nearly every corner of the earth, very few of these rain forest people remain unaffected. Indeed it is these very contacts with Westerners that have been the main factor in reducing the numbers of the rain forest people.

KEY FACTS

- **Rain forest peoples are traditionally nomadic, moving from one area of forest to another to find food.**
- **Rain forest peoples usually manage the forest with great care, never taking more from it than is necessary.**
- **All of today's rain forest peoples are threatened by development and overuse of their rain forest home by outsiders.**

When Westerners arrived in rain forest areas, many of them quickly decided that rain forest peoples were "savages" and that they should take up a Western way of life and religion. Westerners have exploited the forests these peoples lived in by logging and mining minerals such as gold, silver, and iron. They have also unwittingly introduced diseases, such as measles, to which local peoples have no natural resistance, killing them by the thousands. Finally, when rain forest groups have resisted the changes brought by incomers, they have either been killed or relocated. Even today the situation is not much better for most of the rain forest peoples that have survived.

An Arara Indian girl and her pet monkey. The Xingu basin where she lives is in the Amazon rain forest.

Hunter-Gatherers

All the needs of rain forest peoples—food, building materials, clothing, medicines, and ceremonial robes and paints—come from the forest around them. One consequence of this is that any one particular area of forest will run out of one or more of these things and the people living there will have to move on to a new area.

A Mbuti woman prepares dinner in front of the shelter she made herself.

Once the group has moved from a particular area, the group does not return to it for a long time; this gives the animals and plants there time to recover. The length of time an area is occupied and the size of that area determine, to a certain extent, a group's way of life.

Hunter-gatherers rely entirely upon naturally growing plants and wild animals for their food. The rain forest peoples of western Africa, the Penan (PEH-nahn), or Punan, from Borneo, and the Semang from Malaysia, are typical hunter-gatherers. They hunt over an area for a matter of days or weeks, depending on how much game or fruit is around, building simple temporary homes in which to live.

The Mbuti (em-BOO-tee) are hunter-gatherers who have lived for thousands of years in the tropical rain forests of the Ituri Forest region of what is now the Democratic Republic of the Congo in Central Africa. They live in temporary villages of circular homes made with a framework of springy young tree stems covered in large leaves to keep out the rain. From the forest around them, the Mbuti collect edible roots, fruits, and fungi (FUN-jie), their vast knowledge of the forest ensuring they avoid anything that is poisonous. They will also eat termites, which are very rich in protein, and honey when they can find it. When necessary the Mbuti go out into the forest

IN FOCUS

Honey

Like most people, the western African rain forest dwellers love honey, one of the few ways they can obtain sugar in any quantity. To find bee nests in the dense forest, they use an odd little bird, the honeyguide. The bird first finds a bee's nest and then goes to look for someone to guide. With its rasping calls and by fluttering the white on its tail feathers, it leads the men to the nest tree. The men smoke the bees out, take the honey, and leave the honeyguide its reward of beeswax and grubs.

and hunt for larger animals, such as monkeys, to provide more of the protein needed in their diet. Most of the hunting is done by the men, who use bows and arrows. They also make long nets into which women and children drive larger forest animals. Traditionally they also trade for other food items with Bantu peoples living outside the forest.

The few remaining hunter-gatherers of the Penan, or Punan, follow a similar way of life in the dwindling rain forests of Sarawak, on Borneo. Unlike the Mbuti, they use blowpipes for hunting, armed with darts that are tipped with poison.

The Baka (BAH-kah) from the forests of Cameroon are also hunter-gatherers, with a similar way of life to that of the Mbuti. Unlike the Mbuti, over the last few hundred years, some groups have settled down for part of the year and now grow a few starch-rich plants such as manioc and plantains. Others obtain these foods by doing a day's work for members of other peoples who live in villages around the forest. Once the rainy season approaches, however, they begin their wanderings again. They search in particular for mango. The mangoes not only provide the Baka with food, but they also attract other fruit-eating animals. The Baka then hunt these animals, which form an important source of protein in their diet.

A Baka child from a West African rain forest eats a giant beetle larva.

Shifting Cultivators

Some groups in the rain forests of Asia and South America stay in one area for much longer than hunter-gatherers. They build more permanent structures to live in and use simple agriculture to increase their food production. When the time comes, however, they still move on,

IN FOCUS

Spider-Fang Toothpicks

In Venezuela, the land of the Piaroa (pee-ah-ROE-ah) Indians, lives the world's largest spider, the burrow-dwelling goliath tarantula. The female can have a body length of 3 in. (9 cm) and the male can span 10 in. (25 cm) across the legs, the size of a dinner plate. The Piaroa "fish" the spiders from their burrows with a length of vine. The spider, which tastes a bit like crab, is roasted over a fire, and its fangs are used as toothpicks. While preparing their darts, the Piaroa hold a tarantula hunt ceremony (below). The medicine man sitting in the center is wearing a tarantula mask on his head.

leaving their villages and fields to return to forest. These rain forest peoples are called shifting cultivators.

A number of peoples from the Amazon forests cling to this way of life. Much has been written about the Yanomami (ee-on-oe-MA-mee), who live in the border regions between Brazil and Venezuela. The focus of each Yanomami community is a large building called a yano (ee-ON-oe) in which 100 or more people from a number of families may live. Close to each yano is an area of forest from which the trees and other plants have been cleared and burned. It is there that the people grow their crops, mainly manioc and plantains, that form the basis of their diet. They cultivate peach palms, which produce a very popular fruit. Special trips are made into the forest to collect peach palm fruits from long abandoned vegetable plots many miles away.

While cultivation in the plots provides the basic food for the community, hunting and gathering from the forest provide other needs. As far as the Yanomami are concerned, almost anything that is edible will be collected and eaten. The list is almost endless and includes small reptiles such as lizards, many kinds of insects, caterpillars, spiders, frogs, crayfish, and crabs. Like the western African peoples, they also greatly enjoy wild honey when they find it.

Using bows and arrows, the men of the community hunt for animals such as tapir, deer, peccaries (a kind of wild pig), monkeys, agoutis, and birds. The amazing arrows are over 7 feet (2 m) long, and the Yanomami use four different kinds of tips on them, depending on what is being hunted. Even the bows are large, nearly 6 feet (2 m) long, and usually taller than the men who use them. Different types of arrowheads are used for different prey. Two types are used mainly for birds. A sharpened blade arrowhead, which goes deep into the flesh, is used for bigger animals such as tapir. The blade on the arrow makes a deep cut but does not usually kill the animal right away. As it runs off into the forest, the hunters follow the trail of blood, hoping that the animal will collapse and die. Another type of arrowhead is used when hunting monkeys. It is a thin, sharp piece of palm wood that is covered with poison. The poison makes the monkey relax its hold on its tree branch and fall to the ground, from where the hunter can collect it. Some of the poisons that the Yanomami use, such as curare, are also lethal to humans, so they handle their arrows with great care.

Curare is also used by the Piaroa (pee-ah-ROE-ah) Indians who live along the

A Piaroa man navigates his dugout canoe along the upper waters of the Orinoco River in the rain forest of Venezuela. He is apparently well-off because he can afford an outboard motor.

Two Warrau Indian children in their home in the Venezuelan rain forest.

Orinoco River where it borders Venezuela and northeastern Colombia. Instead of hunting with bow and arrow, however, the Piaroa use 10-foot- (3-m-) long blowpipes. Skillful with these weapons, a good hunter can hit prey up to 130 feet (40 m) away. Like the Yanomami the Piaroa live in large, communal houses, around which they clear areas of forest to create farms called *kanukus* (KAH-noo-koos), which all members of the community usually share.

The Tikuna (TEE-koo-nah) also live in the Amazon rain forest. Their way of life is much like that of the Piaroa or the Yanomami. However, they depend more upon the large rivers to provide food, traveling in dugout canoes that may be as long as 40 feet (12 m). These are made by hollowing out a tree trunk and then suspending it over a fire. The flames soften the wood, allowing the Tikuna to mold the canoe into its final shape. Many

IN FOCUS

Big Feet

Most rain forest peoples have little fear and much skill when it comes to climbing tall trees to collect fruit or honey. While some of them use straps around the tree trunk to help them climb, the Yanomami and some of the peoples from Papua New Guinea seem able to shin straight up a tree with no such aids. It seems that these people have particularly wide feet with splayed-out toes. These not only help them to climb but also prevent them from sinking too far into the mud on the forest floor.

Tikuna women keep tiny marmoset monkeys as pets and walk around with them on their heads as a sort of decoration.

Much of New Guinea is covered by rain forest inhabited by many different peoples. Like the rain forest dwellers of other parts of the world, the way they live today has been altered by their contact with Westerners, especially missionaries. There still remain, however, one or two relatively untouched groups deep in the forest who combine simple agriculture with hunting and gathering. One such group is the Kaluli (KAH-loo-lee), who live in the Southern Highlands Province of Papua New Guinea. The Kaluli live by farming in forest clearings, supplementing their diet by hunting small prey such as lizards and rodents, as well as fish and crayfish from streams.

IN FOCUS

Cosmetics from the Forest

Many rain forest peoples enjoy decorating both their face and their body, often with extremely complicated and colorful patterns. Such body and face art is used decoratively among many groups but is also a feature at important ceremonies such as weddings or funerals, for hunting, or when going to war. The paints that they use come from the mud and various plant juices available in the forest.

What About the Future?

It is very unlikely that in the future the world will have any room for the rain forest peoples. Already much of their forest home is gone, and it continues to disappear at a rapid rate. In some countries these people appear to be considered an embarrassment. They are being forced to leave the forest and to live in a "civilized" way like other people. Unable to cope with the outside world's way of life, they fall easy victims to drugs and alcohol.

In the past, most of the rain forest peoples have treated the forests around them as divine, since it provided them

In Kalimantan in Indonesia, this old Dyak man has been converted to Christianity.

with all their needs. They treated the forest with great respect, apologizing to an animal when they killed it or to a tree when they cut it down. Today most of them have been visited by missionaries, who have slowly converted these rain forest peoples to Western religions.

Despite introducing new diseases that have decimated the populations of rain forest groups around the world, Westerners have improved the health of some rain forest peoples. To some extent these peoples are now able to obtain drugs to combat diseases such as malaria, and some can even obtain simple hospital treatment. They have the benefit of modern metal tools and guns, which make hunting easier, though many still prefer their blowpipes or bows and arrows.

The future of the rain forest peoples, however, lies in the hands of the young. If they wish to go on with the old ways and traditions—and fight for them if necessary—then their culture may survive. If they decide to leave the forest and enter the "modern" world, then the rain forest peoples and their special way of life will soon be no more.

Check these out:

Disease • **Dyak People** • **Exploitation** • **Homes in the Rain Forest** • **Hunter-Gatherer** • **Kaluli People** • **Kayapo People** • **Kuna People** • **Makah People** • **Maya People** • **Mbuti People** • **Miskito People** • **Quinault People** • **Resettlement** • **Tlingit People** • **Yanomami People**

Photosynthesis

Photosynthesis is the process by which green plants make their own food from simple materials. Except for some bacteria, no other living organisms can do this—they all have to get their food from existing plant or animal matter.

Photosynthesis is a very complex process, taking place in several stages and involving many chemical reactions. Carbon dioxide and water are combined, with the help of sunlight, to form a simple sugar called glucose. The glucose produced by photosynthesis provides all the energy needed for living and growing, and it is the starting point for everything else needed by the plant. Large numbers of glucose molecules link up to form cellulose, which is the main building material in the plant kingdom.

Glucose is also combined with minerals absorbed from the soil to form proteins, which are essential components of all living matter. Many plants store starch or sugar, both of which are made from glucose. When we eat

KEY FACTS

- ***Photosynthesis* means "making with light." It can be carried out only by green plants in the presence of light.**
- **Dark-colored leaves are better at absorbing light than pale ones.**

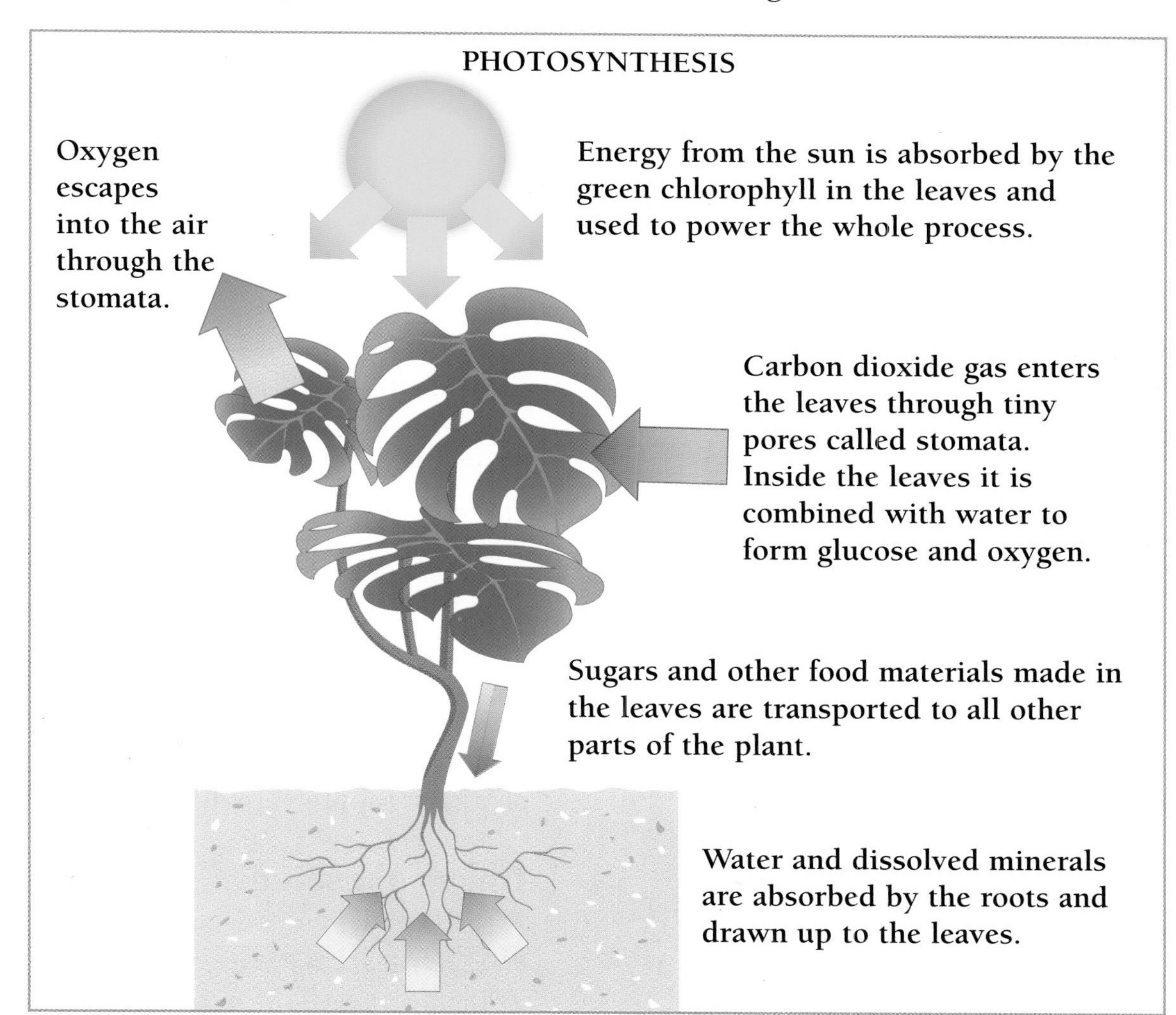

vegetables or other plant food, we get energy from the starch or sugar, and we use the proteins to build up our own bodies. In one way or another, almost all life on Earth relies on photosynthesis to provide its food.

Water, Light, and Air

Photosynthesis takes place mainly in the leaves of a plant. The carbon dioxide is absorbed from the air through microscopic pores called stomata, which occur mainly on the undersides of the leaves. Oxygen also escapes through the stomata. Although rain forest epiphytes soak up a lot of water through their leaves, the trees get most of their water from the soil through their roots. Water is drawn up to the leaves—often hundreds of feet above the roots—by a process called transpiration. As water vapor escapes through the stomata, more water is drawn from the leaf veins to take its place. The suction generated by the evaporation of water from all the leaves is enough to pull water all the way up from the roots.

IN FOCUS

Dark Secrets

Down on the forest floor, the few green plants that manage to survive there have special features that allow them to cope with the low light levels. They generally have large, dark leaves, because dark colors are better at absorbing light than pale ones. The dark colors are often produced by red pigments mixed with the chlorophyll. These red pigments absorb light more efficiently than chlorophyll, but then they pass their energy to the chlorophyll. The undersides of some rain forest plants, such as the African violet, are quite red.

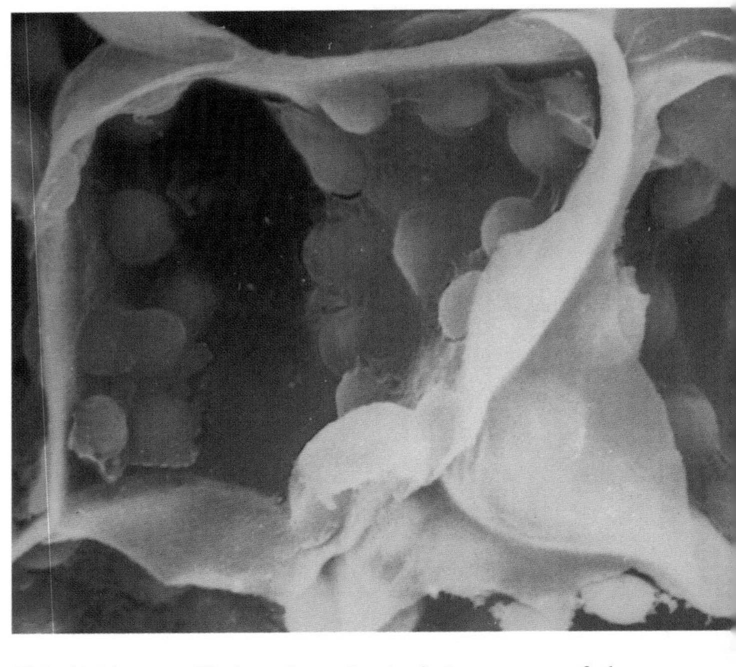

This highly magnified section of a leaf shows some of the individual cells of which it is made. The round blobs fixed to the walls of the cells are chloroplasts—the packets of chorophyll in which photosynthesis takes place.

Although most of this water escapes into the air as water vapor, the leaf cells soak up what they need for photosynthesis.

Essential Sunlight

The energy needed for photosynthesis comes from sunlight, which is trapped by the green chlorophyll in the leaves. The energy in the sunlight is converted to chemical energy during photosynthesis and is eventually stored in the glucose. The need for sunlight explains why a plant's leaves are generally arranged in a sort of mosaic, with no leaf completely shaded by another. There are very few gaps in the rain forest canopy: the leaves are arranged to intercept almost all of the light.

Check these out:

● Dormancy ● Food Web ● Flowering Plant ● Leaf ● Plant ● Root ● Shade Toleration ● Tree

Pig and Peccary

Pigs and peccaries are hoofed mammals with short legs, thick bodies, large heads, and short necks. Their long snouts end in a flat disk. Wild pigs are found throughout the Tropics outside the Americas, but domesticated pigs have been introduced to Central and South America. Peccaries are like medium-sized pigs with more slender legs. They live in Central and South America. "Hog" is simply another name for pig.

KEY FACTS

- **In many places, pigs and peccaries are hunted because they are pests. Collared peccaries and African bushpigs will eat their way through fields of crops, and African wild pigs are prone to sleeping sickness and swine fever.**
- **When danger threatens, adult peccaries shelter their young between their legs.**
- **The bearded pig of Southeast Asia allows crowned wood partridges to pick ticks off its skin. The partridges are also useful for alerting the pigs to danger by their loud calls.**

A Nose for Food

Most wild pigs and some peccaries are nocturnal or feed mainly at dawn and dusk. The pig's snout is loaded with smell and touch sensors, and a large part of a pig's brain deals with analyzing smells. The snout is constantly moving, sniffing the air or rooting in moist earth and leaf litter for roots, bulbs, and fallen fruits. Pigs are omnivores: they eat a range of foods, from fungi (FUN-jie), ferns, and leaves to grubs, worms, mice, and even frogs. Peccaries will also eat carrion, the remains of dead animals.

Pigs and peccaries use scent to communicate, too. Some have special scent glands in front of their eyes or near their lips or feet, which they use to mark trees, logs, and rocks in their territories. They also mark each other so that they can recognize members of their own group.

Peccaries also have a scent gland on their back, which produces a strong musky odor. An excited or angry peccary will erect the mane of hair on its neck and give off an unpleasant smell. The dung of pigs and peccaries also carries a personal scent message.

The babirusa's huge tusks curve back to reach its forehead, but they are more for show than for fighting.

The giant forest hog from Africa has two pairs of tusks. The larger pair is used for digging; the smaller, sharper pair for fighting.

Tasks for Tusks

All pigs and peccaries have large, tusklike canine teeth that curve upward and outward. Males have the biggest tusks. These are powerful weapons, effective enough to fight off leopards, tigers, or jaguars, or other males competing for females. The babirusa of Sulawesi has huge tusks that grow straight up through the skin of its snout and curve back so that they sometimes reach its forehead. Such a shape is not much use for fighting but may well impress other males and, more importantly, females.

Many pigs have tough skin, fleshy shoulder pads, and large warts on their faces to protect them against their opponents' tusks and from thorns that brush them as they run through the forest. The giant forest hog of western Africa sports dual-purpose tusks—the long upper tusks help it dig for roots while the smaller lower ones are actually its main fighting weapons.

Home Life

Most pigs live in groups called sounders, made up of a mother (sow) and her piglets, and sometimes some older daughters, too. Adult males usually live alone but sometimes form roving bachelor groups. The strongest males get to mate with the females.

Collared peccaries live in family groups of up to five animals, including a male, a female, and young. These groups may combine with others to form bigger herds. White-lipped peccaries form large herds of over 100 individuals. To reduce tension and fighting between the adult males in such groups, there is a distinct hierarchy; displays of strength and contests sort out which are the top peccaries.

When not foraging, pigs and peccaries usually hide out in thickets or dens. Some species, like the giant forest hog, live in the same dens for generations, gradually extending them and the series of tunnel-like paths they trample to their favorite feeding grounds.

IN FOCUS

Planting Seeds

Churned-up leaves and soil on the forest floor are clues that there are pigs or peccaries around. Many pigs actually bury seeds, helping to disperse them. Other seeds are scattered in their droppings when the pigs have eaten fruit. By loosening soil with their snouts, pigs let air into the soil and make it easier for seeds to germinate.

Check these out:
Mammal · Migration

Piranha

Rivaling sharks in their notoriety, South America's piranhas have a reputation for frenzied killing sprees and are said to be able to devour humans and other large mammals. Most piranhas, however, are small fish that feed on even smaller fish and on carrion (dead animal remains). The most dangerous species, the "true piranhas," are the largest, up to 2 feet (60 cm) long.

Piranhas are black or silvery fish, often with orange bellies and throats. They have deep bodies, sharp-edged bellies, and large, blunt heads. Their razor-sharp teeth have a scissorlike bite, and their large skulls have enough space to accommodate powerful jaw muscles.

Feeding Frenzies

Piranhas gather in huge numbers wherever there is a commotion in the water. The scent of blood also attracts them. Individual piranhas dart in and out of the seething mass of fish, biting off chunks of the victim's flesh. By devouring sick and injured fish, piranhas help to keep the remaining fish stocks healthy.

Piranhas will attack humans in the water, but in most cases the human will have died of drowning before the fish attack. However, piranhas still attack injured people who fall into the water, especially if the fish are short of food.

Humans are also enemies of piranhas. Piranhas make excellent sport fish, putting up a challenging fight when hooked, and their firm, white flesh is thought to be tasty. In the past they have been surprisingly popular aquarium fish, but many states have now prohibited their importation, for fear that the fish will escape and breed in U.S. waters.

In parts of the Orinoco River basin in South America, where floods prevent villagers from burying their dead for part of the year, corpses are left in the water. Piranhas eat the flesh, and the cleaned skeletons are decorated and buried when the floods recede. Piranha teeth are so sharp that some South American Indian people use them as scissors.

The importation of piranhas has now been banned in many states.

Check these out:

Fish • Fishing • Pollution • River

Pirarucu

The pirarucu, also known as the arapaima and the paiche, lives in the Amazon and neighboring rivers of South America, where more than half of the world's freshwater fishes are found. One of the world's largest freshwater fish, some pirarucu specimens are rumored to have reached a length of about 14 feet (4 m) and a weight of about 450 pounds (200 kg). However, individuals more than about 7 feet (2 m) long are very rare. This may be because the indigenous people of Amazonia catch so many for food that few get a chance to grow to their maximum size.

The pirarucu is one of the few surviving members of an ancient family that has been in existence for over 100 million years. It is largely green, with a reddish tinge toward the back. The male's tail becomes bright red in the breeding season. Bony plates cover the small head, and the scales are also bony and much thicker than those of most other fishes. The dorsal and anal fins are all the way back and almost join the tail fin. These three fins drive the great fish slowly forward when the tail moves from side to side.

The large body scales and the bony armor on the head are easily seen on these pirarucu.

The pirarucu lives mainly in the shallow, slow-moving waters at the river's edge. It can survive in stagnant water that contains little oxygen because it has a large air bladder that opens into its throat and acts like a lung. The fish comes to the surface to take a gulp of air. It feeds mainly on other fishes but also eats water snails, crustaceans, turtles, frogs, snakes, and fruit that has fallen into the water.

During the breeding season, the male and female dig several nests in the sand in shallow water. The female can lay nearly 200,000 eggs each year.

Check these out:
Amazonia · Fish · Fishing · River

Plants dominate the world's rain forests. They provide a wide range of habitats, homes, shelters, and food for animals. The dense vegetation captures moisture, preventing floods and soil erosion, and traps nutrients. Even dead plants rot down and replenish the soil. The thick layer of dead leaves, flowers, and fallen tree trunks provides homes and food for many tiny animals, from worms and slugs to beetles and millipedes.

Tropical rain forests have a greater variety of plants than any other place on Earth. There are trees, shrubs, climbers, scramblers, epiphytes, parasites, underwater plants, and even carnivorous plants. Flowering plants mingle with cycads, ferns, club mosses, and mosses. Trees are draped with lianas (lee-AH-nuhs), mosses, and hanging gardens of ferns and orchids. Mosses may cover old leaves.

KEY FACTS

- **The vegetation in a rain forest is extremely dense: as little as one percent of the sunlight that falls on the canopy reaches the ground below.**
- **Woody vines called lianas bind the great trees together. Some lianas grow up to 330 ft. (about 100 m) long and may be 2 ft. (60 cm) in diameter.**
- **There are about 220,000 species of flowering plants (50,000 of them tropical trees), 530 different conifers, 10,000 ferns, 16,600 mosses, 1,000 club mosses, and 185 cycads.**

What Is a Plant?

A plant makes its own food, using carbon dioxide from the air and water and minerals from the soil. It uses the energy of sunlight, absorbed by its leaves, to build these simple starting materials into the complex tissues of the plant body in a process called photosynthesis.

Plant cells have walls made of cellulose, which is flexible enough to allow the cells to bend as the plant sways in the wind or when animals walk over it. The cell walls can stretch to become firm as the cells swell with water, like the air in a bicycle tire makes the tire hard. Older plants lay down tough fibers to form wood for extra support.

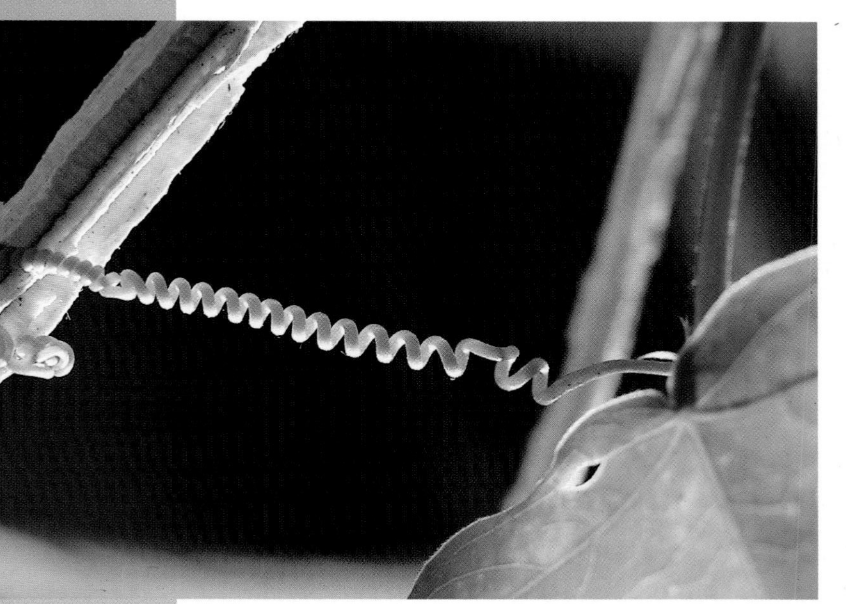

A tendril grows out between a leaf and the stem of a passionflower vine. These tendrils grow almost straight until they touch a support, then they coil tightly to make a firm anchor.

Rain Forest Leaves

Most rain forest trees are green year-round. They renew their leaves a few at a time, not all at once.

Although they may be evergreen, many rain forest trees produce new leaves in bursts every few months. This helps the tree because insects that would eat young leaves do not get a chance to multiply too fast if their food supply stays limited. In places where there are distinct dry seasons, trees may shed all their leaves for a short time.

Shiny leaves with long pointed tips—drip tips—are common in rain forests. Rain runs off them quickly, dripping from the long tip. It rinses off the spores of fungi (FUN-jie) and mosses that might otherwise grow on the leaves and that could cut off the light needed for photosynthesis.

High in the canopy, where branches are more exposed to sun and wind, leaves are often quite small and simple. They have a small surface area to reduce water loss. In the moist shade below the canopy, water loss is not a problem, so leaves are larger to absorb as much light as possible. In the darker parts of the forest, divided leaves are more common.

Reaching for the Sun

Since plants make their food by photosynthesis, they need light to grow. The plants in a rain forest all compete for light. The tallest trees, the emergents, have their crowns in full sunlight, but they have to grow up to it first.

Many plants cheat: they grow on other plants, so they save energy by not having to grow so tall. Scramblers have stiff leaves or stems with backward thorns that act like grappling hooks to keep them from slipping as they grow over other plants, sneaking ever upward. Many climbing bamboos and climbing palms have spiky stems, and often spiky leaves, too, to help them move upward.

Climbers such as morning glories use twining stems to wind their way up other plants. The passionflower vines of the Americas, Asia, and the Pacific have long tendrils that emerge where the leaves join the stem. When they touch another plant, they twine tightly around it.

Other climbers, such as the peperomias with their candlelike flowers, put out little suckerlike roots from their stems. Delicate

A West Indian vine, Marantia, *uses other plants for support. Many such vines are highly prized by gardeners for their attractive flowers.*

A bromeliad seedling has managed to germinate on the surface of an old leaf, which has lost much of its shiny wax coating. Water running off glossy younger leaves would have washed the seed away.

filmy ferns anchor themselves in this way to shady buttress roots and smooth, damp tree trunks.

Tall climbers, like the strange, ropelike lianas that climb all the way up to the canopy, have a long way to carry water from their roots to their leaves. Lianas have extra-wide water-carrying tubes running up their stems. Water evaporating from their large crowns of leaves exerts a powerful suction, pulling water up the stem. If a liana stem is cut, air is sucked into it so fast that it hisses, and clear, drinkable water will run out of it.

Plants on Plants

Many orchids and bromeliads (broe-MEE-lee-ads) start life high in the forest: their seeds germinate on branches and in the crevices of tree trunks. Their roots absorb moisture and dissolved minerals that percolate down the bark. Scrambler figs start life as seedlings high on a branch in the canopy but send down incredibly long roots to the forest floor.

Even leaves and stems may be covered in mosses, lichens, filmy ferns, and algae. Plants that grow on leaves are called epiphylls. Mosses and lichens cover almost every exposed plant surface, except very shiny leaves. Being small and quite slow-growing, they do not need big supplies of water or nutrients, so they can survive in cracks and crevices in tree bark and even on the worn surfaces of old leaves.

Some plants, such as rafflesia (ruh-FLEE-zee-uh), feed on other plants, sending out little suckers into their tissues. Others feed on dead and decaying plant material or on fungi. Carnivorous plants trap insects and digest their juices.

IN FOCUS

Not a Plant

Fungi, lichens, and algae are often thought of as plants, but they are not. Fungi do not photosynthesize, and their cell walls are not made of cellulose. Lichens are strange associations between fungi and algae. Algae are plantlike organisms that do photosynthesize, but they do not have stems or leaves. Most are simple organisms, either single cells or little chains or clusters of cells. In rain forest pools, lakes, and streams, millions of algae float near the water's surface in the light. They form the base of the food chain: the tiny algae are eaten by fish and invertebrates, which in turn are eaten by larger fish, and so on. Other algae live in the moisture that covers plants and soil particles, where they also support tiny food chains.

Plants with "Knees"
The rain forest is at its thickest along the banks of rivers and lakes, where the extra light fuels a great tangle of shrubs and creepers. Slow-moving rivers and quiet lakes have their own rich plant life. However, life at the water's edge is not all that easy. Plant roots need oxygen, and waterlogged soil does not contain much. Waterside plants have large air canals in their stems to let oxygen move from the leaves to the roots. Swamp trees, such as many mangroves, may have "knees"—roots that grow up out of the swampy ground into the air—or prop roots that grow from the trunk down to the ground. The corky covering of these roots is full of tiny holes to let oxygen in.

The thick woody stems of lianas form fantastic shapes as they coil from tree to tree. This one is in the Bwindi Impenetrable Forest National Park in Uganda.

Another problem for plants is flooding. Fed by rain from distant mountains, rain forest rivers can suddenly swell and submerge the plants that fringe them, tearing off leaves and branches. Some riverside plants, such as palms, have long, ribbonlike leaves that allow the water to flow between them, reducing the risk of damage. In the Amazon some areas are flooded for more than half the year, often to depths of several feet. Nobody really understands how the plants of the understory and forest floor survive in such places.

IN FOCUS

Poisonous Passionflowers

Passionflowers are found throughout the Tropics. They have poisons in their tissues to protect them from plant-eating insects. A few insects, however, can cope with these poisons and actually use them for their own defense. Heliconiid butterflies flock to passionflowers to lay their eggs on the leaves. The poisons build up in their caterpillars' bodies as they feed on the leaves, so the butterflies too are poisonous and unpleasant to taste. Some passionflower vines produce tiny egglike structures on their leaves. When a heliconiid sees these, it thinks another butterfly has already laid its eggs there, so it moves on to look for another vine. In this way there will never be too many caterpillars feeding on the vine.

Moving Out
It is important for young plants to grow far from their parents. If seeds or spores germinate too close to their parent plant, they will be unable to grow in its shade, and they will be competing with its giant roots for nutrients and water.

Wind, water, or animals carry away seeds or spores. Mosses and ferns produce spores, which are much smaller than seeds and contain very little stored food. This means it does not cost the plant much energy and nutrients to produce large numbers of them, and they are small and light enough to be carried on air currents.

Some plants use air or water to carry their seeds away. The kapok, or ceiba (SAE-buh) tree of South America releases its seeds in great balls of cottony fluff that float on air currents between times of flooding. If they land in a river, they drift downstream until they are washed ashore. Other trees encase their seeds in fleshy fruits that attract animals, including fish and bats. The animals eat the fruits, and the seeds pass unharmed through their bodies and are deposited some distance away in their droppings.

Living Under Water

The giant water lilies of the Amazon and the lotus flowers found throughout the Tropics are rooted in the mud far below the water's surface. Their huge leaves, up to 7 feet (2 m) across, support birds such as jacanas and provide them with their own private nesting rafts. The leaves contain many air spaces and float at the surface. When the water rises, their stems grow rapidly, up to 8 inches (20 cm) a day. When the water falls, the leaves and stems may be left high and dry, but the roots survive, and new stems sprout when the floods return.

Growing in parts of the floodplains where the river water is moving slowly, are vast floating meadows and rafts of plants, some of them up to a mile (over a kilometer) long. They trap mud and plant debris, where other plants, such as passionflower vines, morning glories, sedges, and even small trees and shrubs, can take root.

These meadows, with their rich vegetation and plentiful seeds, are home to over 100 species of fish. They are important nurseries for young fish, providing both food and shelter, hiding them from the eyes of birds and other predators. As they drift slowly downstream, the floating meadows carry with them frogs, birds, and a host of invertebrates.

The leaves of the giant Amazon water lily are up to 7 ft. (2 m) wide. Birds can walk across them, and even build their nests on them.

Check these out:

- Bromeliad
- Climber
- Dormancy
- Emergent
- Epiphyte
- Fern
- Flowering Plant
- Leaf
- Light Gap
- Mangrove Forest
- Medicinal Plant
- Nutrient Cycle
- Orchid
- Palm Tree
- Photosynthesis
- Pollination
- Rafflesia
- Rain Forest
- Root
- Rubber Tree
- Seed
- Shade Toleration
- Tree

Plantation

Visit many areas today that were once covered in rain forest, and you will find that, over thousands of acres, they are covered in plantations of a single plant species. The island of St. Lucia in the Caribbean, for example, once had large areas of rain forest, but banana plantations have now replaced almost all of them. These are of course not just for the inhabitants to eat but are exported to the richer nations of the world. Huge areas of rain forest in other parts of the world have been cleared to grow plantations of rubber trees and oil palms. Palm oil forms the basis of margarines and cooking oils and has many other uses. Rubber trees produce latex to make rubber. In the past, as the rubber plantations aged and the trees were replaced, the old ones were burned. Today rubber-tree wood is used to make durable flooring for homes in the Western world.

KEY FACTS

- **Plantations are usually monocultures—they contain just one species or variety of plant.**
- **Not all plantations require the rain forest to be cleared, because some crops need to be grown in the shade of larger rain forest trees.**

Some plants, such as coffee and cocoa, grow better under the shade of larger rain forest trees. These crops have a less damaging impact upon the rain forest because the natural tree canopy can be left in place, and native mammals, birds, and insects can still thrive there. However, coffee bushes that do not need shade have now been developed, and these can be planted in clear-felled

Huge areas of rain forest have been felled in order to satisfy the world demand for bananas. This plantation is in western Malaysia.

A plantation of young teak trees in southern India. It is hoped that such plantations will reduce the need for further felling of the world's rain forests.

areas, making life much easier for the plantation owner but destroying the rain forest in the process.

Tree Plantations

However, some plantations are more eco-friendly. It has been calculated that if all of the world's damaged rain forest areas were planted with commercial species of trees, then they would produce enough wood for today's global market. This would mean that not a single piece of primary rain forest would need to be felled ever again. Logging devastates rain forests. It requires roads to be cut into the forest, as well as a great deal of labor and machinery. For this reason, it makes sense to grow large areas of a single tree species. Then they can be tended more easily, and the distances to harvest the wood reduced.

Eucalyptus plantations are springing up in places such as Madagascar to produce wood for making furniture and charcoal and for firewood. Although not a native tree, it appears that the lemurs endemic to Madagascar find it appealing, since some species enter the plantations to feed on the flowers.

Teak, an important wood for making high-quality furniture, is now grown in plantations in felled Indian monsoon forest. These plantations are not as environmentally beneficial as the eucalyptus, since the trees are planted close together to make them grow straight. They also have large leaves that, when they fall, form a thick carpet through which other plants are unable to grow. These types of plantations are gradually being adopted, but whether or not they will be used widely enough to save most of the remaining rain forest is unknown.

IN FOCUS

Village Plantations

Living miles from any supplies of electricity or natural gas, rain forest dwellers have to rely upon fires to cook their food. This often involves traveling long distances to find suitable wood and damages the forest. Today in many rain forest areas such as Madagascar, people are encouraged to grow a plantation of eucalyptus trees close to the village. These grow quickly and produce good firewood.

Check these out:

- Central America
- Deforestation
- Exploitation
- Forestry
- Reforestation

Poaching

Poaching means hunting animals in areas where they are protected by law. Poaching was first made a criminal offense around the 10th century in Europe to protect the stocks of game animals (animals hunted for sport and food) on private land. Punishments were severe, ranging from the confiscation of the poachers' weapons and tools, such as guns and snares, to the mutilation of their dogs or of the poachers themselves, and even death.

KEY FACTS

- **In part of western Africa, people kill gorillas and other primates for food.**
- **Poachers often kill many "protected" animals and then sell their parts as souvenirs to tourists.**
- **In Papua New Guinea, local people now protect the birds of paradise that share their rain forest home.**

The game reserves established around the beginning of the 20th century in Africa were designed to protect sport hunting. Local people were stopped from hunting the animals that were the favorite targets of white hunters. At this time hunters from Europe had no idea that the vast herds they were hunting could ever be reduced. They killed lions, buffalo, rhinoceroses, and elephants, mainly for trophies but often for the profit to be made from selling horns and ivory—the beginnings of the vast international trade in animal parts that was later to endanger many large African species. Many of these game reserves

This forest guide in Rwanda has found a trap set to catch gorillas for bush meat and souvenirs.

IN FOCUS: A Poisonous Trade

Among the more unlikely victims of systematic poaching in the Amazon rain forest and in Costa Rica were poison dart frogs. Collectors in Europe, especially in Germany, would pay high prices for these potentially dangerous pets. The trade was effectively destroyed by conservationists in Europe, who bred from frogs confiscated in customs until they became so common—and cheap—that it was no longer worth hunting them in the wild.

later became parks to protect wildlife. Understandably local people resented being banned from hunting for food on their own native lands.

The resentment at being excluded from once-communal land still persists among many groups of people, and not just in Africa. However, poaching is a symptom of a more difficult problem afflicting rain forest countries: poverty. Rain forest peoples have always had respect for the animals and plants of the forest, and for the most part they have not taken more from their environment than they needed. However, hunger and poverty have pushed other local people, and their governments, to exploit the valuable resources of the rain forests until they run out. Although most game reserves have now been set aside as national parks, poaching is still a regular event, sometimes committed even by the very people that have been hired to protect the forest and its animals.

Bush Meat

There are two main kinds of poaching in the modern world, and both are found in the rain forest as well as elsewhere. The first, and most common, is hunting for

Wildlife products for sale to tourists in Myanmar. The beautiful skin is from a clouded leopard, classified as a vulnerable species.

Mangabeys and a red river hog from the forest on sale as bush meat in an African market.

food. All over the world, where hunter-gatherers survive, they need to be able to hunt as their ancestors did, without being prevented by laws designed to protect rare species. In many places the local people have proved to be the best guardians of these rare species.

In Nigeria professional hunters regularly kill several rare species of primates, such as mangabeys and guenons (GWE-nuhns), to sell in the local markets. In other parts of western Africa, gorillas are threatened with extinction from being killed for food as well as for tourist trophies.

This bush meat trade has always gone on: the difference now is that the demand has become enormous because civil war and the movement of large numbers of people have disrupted agriculture and forced people to leave their homes, fleeing to the forests for safety. The huge number of modern firearms left over from wars provide a way to meet this increased demand for bush meat. It is sometimes difficult to convince local people that these animals, which they have seen around them and have eaten all their lives, need protecting.

Souvenirs

The other reason for poaching animals is to satisfy the demand for colorful souvenirs for tourists to take home and to supply an international, multimillion-dollar trade in animal skins, ivory, and live specimens. Butterfly wings from the rain forests of Malaysia or Myanmar, or feathers from

New Guinea's birds of paradise are things that thoughtless people will buy as "mementos" of their travels. Rain forest animals, such as elephants and tigers, are valuable victims of international poaching, and the steady drain on their numbers is having a serious effect.

IN FOCUS

Poaching Plants

Poaching also includes the removal of rare plants from the forest. Most countries now forbid the export of orchids, for example, because too many of them have been collected and sold overseas.

Poaching Trees

A more destructive form of poaching involves stealing the forest itself. As more and more protected areas are established in the rain forest, the same resentment has grown against this exclusion as against the ban on hunting. In areas as far apart as the Philippines and Central America, and also in Malaysia and Myanmar, local people see no reason why they should not be able to use the forest as they always have. Clearing and burning to produce farmland is harmful enough, but people also fell rare and valuable trees to sell illegally to timber merchants. Ebony in Africa, mahogany in Central America, and sandalwood in India are all examples of trees that are so valuable that poachers consider it worth the risk of discovery and arrest to fell them at night and remove them from protected areas.

A monkey hunter in Sierra Leone with his victims, spot-nosed monkeys, destined for the bush meat market.

Check these out:

- Careers
- Congo
- Endangered Species
- Exploitation
- Gorilla
- Human Interference

Pollination

Unlike animals, plants cannot move around in search of a suitable mate. To make seeds and reproduce, plants have to be pollinated. This is the process whereby pollen grains containing male cells are transported from the stamens to the female parts of the flowers, known as the carpels. These are usually right in the center of the flower, and in many flowers they are surrounded by the stamens. The pollen has to reach a special area of the carpel known as the stigma. Designed to trap the pollen grains, this is on top of the carpel and often carried on a little stalk. Male cells from the pollen grains then enter the carpels and fertilize the female cells. Each fertilized cell can then grow into a seed. The same thing happens in conifers, except that the pollen and the female cells are produced in cones.

KEY FACTS

- **A hummingbird can drink up to nine times its own weight in nectar each day. This means visiting well over a thousand flowers.**
- **An orchid in Madagascar hides its nectar in a tube about a foot (30 cm) long. Its only pollinator is the hawkmoth, which has a tongue about the same length.**
- **The flowers of lantana and some other plants change color after pollination so that insects will not bother to visit them any more.**

BIRD POLLINATION

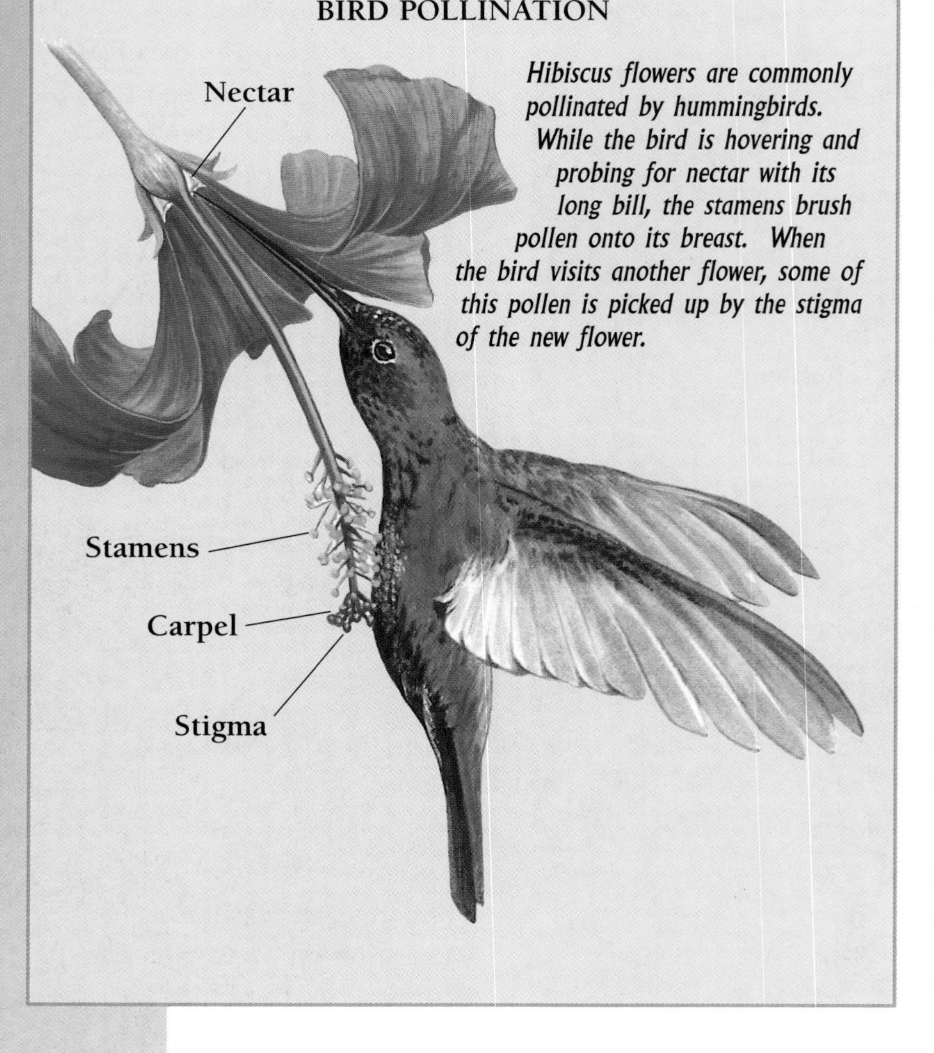

Hibiscus flowers are commonly pollinated by hummingbirds. While the bird is hovering and probing for nectar with its long bill, the stamens brush pollen onto its breast. When the bird visits another flower, some of this pollen is picked up by the stigma of the new flower.

Self-Pollination and Cross-Pollination

Self-pollination is the transfer of pollen from the stamens to the stigmas of the same flower or to another flower on the same plant. Cross-pollination is when a flower's pollen is carried to a flower of the same kind but growing on a different plant. Cross-pollination is much better than self-pollination

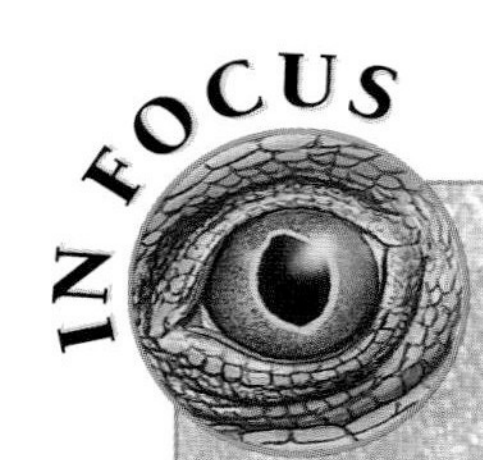

Staggered Opening Hours

When many different kinds of plants flower at the same time, much of their pollen is wasted because it gets carried to the wrong kind of flower. Some flowers that share the same pollinators avoid this problem by opening at different times of the year, or simply at different times of the day. Various kinds of African acacia trees, for example, release their pollen at different times of day, so although they are all visited by the same kinds of bees, there is a good chance that the pollen will end up in the right kind of flower.

because it can produce stronger offspring and more variety. Many flowers have developed some way of preventing or at least discouraging self-pollination. Stamens and stigmas often ripen at different times to cut down the chance of self-pollination, and some flowers have chemical barriers that prevent their own pollen from getting into their own carpels. Some species produce pollen and carpels on separate male and female plants, and then there is absolutely no possibility of self-pollination.

Wind and water pollinate many plants, transporting pollen from one plant to another. However, wind pollination is not effective in the rain forest because there are so many leaves that get in the way. Rain forest plants, therefore, rely mainly on insects, birds, and bats. Small monkeys and other primates may also pollinate some rain forest flowers. Even some of the grasses, which are normally pollinated by the wind, are pollinated by flies and bees in the rain forests.

Pollination by Insects

Large bees, especially those known as carpenter bees, are the main insects involved in pollinating rain forest flowers. They are joined by butterflies, moths, beetles, flies, and many much smaller insects. Moth-pollinated flowers are generally pale, and they usually open and emit their scent only at night. Bright colors and scents attract other insects, and most flowers also provide sweet nectar for their visitors. Flowers pollinated by butterflies, moths, and bees are often tubular, and the insects have to probe deeply for the nectar with their long

While this honeybee probes for nectar, the pale stamens on the right of the flower dust its back with pollen.

tongues. While sipping the nectar, the insects become dusted with pollen, usually in just the right place for it to rub against the stigma of the next flower to be visited. Bees collect large amounts of pollen, which they feed to their grubs, but there is always enough for pollination as well. The flowers of many rain forest trees produce extra pollen for the bees instead of nectar.

Pollination by Birds

Many rain forest birds regularly drink nectar, pollinating flowers while doing so. They usually have very slender beaks with which they probe deeply into the flowers. Nectar-feeding birds cannot live in the cooler parts of the world because there are too few flowers in the winter.

Bird-pollinated flowers are often red or orange—colors that seem particularly attractive to birds—but they do not have much scent because birds in general have a poor sense of smell. The flowers tend to be long and tubular, and they often hang well away from the leaves so that the birds can see them easily. They produce lots of watery nectar that the birds suck up with their long tongues or beaks. Hummingbirds, which are the best known of the pollinating birds in the American rain forests, have slender beaks that are often longer than the rest of their bodies, and their tubular tongues are even longer. The birds hover in front of or below the flowers while feeding.

Pollination by Bats

Bat-pollinated flowers open at night and usually have pale colors and strong scents. They are often borne on the trunks or larger branches of plants, where they are not concealed by the leaves. Tufts of stamens generally scatter pollen all over the visiting bats while they lap up the sticky nectar. Durians and bananas are commonly pollinated by bats.

A long-nosed bat about to lap nectar from a bird-of-paradise flower. The stamens protrude from the purple part of the flower and dust the bat's belly with pollen.

Check these out:

Bat • Bee and Wasp • Bird • Feeding • Flowering Plant • Fruit • Herbivore • Insect • Plant • Seed

Pollution

Pollution is the buildup of substances put into the environment by humans. The substances are called pollutants. The major sources of pollution are burning fossil fuels in engines and power plants, waste disposal, accidental spills of chemicals from factories, and the use of agricultural chemicals on farms. The three main types of pollution are air pollution, water pollution, and land pollution. All these types of pollution may affect the world's rain forests.

KEY FACTS

- **Pollution is the buildup of substances in the environment that cannot be broken down by natural processes.**
- **In Colombia illegal drug-processing plants release kerosene and sulfuric acid into the environment.**
- **Mercury poisoning, a result of gold mining, is a serious problem in the Amazon River basin.**

Besides being unsightly, most types of pollution are a hazard to the lives of plants and animals, including humans. The effects of some, such as oil spills, are seen immediately; the effects of others, such as the buildup of carbon dioxide believed to cause global warming, are only obvious decades after they begin.

Pollution is a major problem in some rain forests. Most of these problems are created by the activities of miners, loggers, and oil companies.

Even people who visit the rain forest for its beauty pollute it. This litter has been dumped at the side of a road used by tourists to reach the Cameron Highlands in Malaysia.

Polluting the Land

Pollutants build up in the environment when they cannot be easily broken down by natural processes. For example, if a tree dies and falls to the ground, microorganisms in the soil gradually break down the wood into the simple chemicals that were its components. These chemicals are then used by other trees. Substances that break down naturally are called biodegradable. When a plastic bag falls to the ground, microorganisms cannot break down its component chemicals, and the bag stays where it is, perhaps forever. Substances that do not break down naturally are called nonbiodegradable.

Most land pollutants are nonbiodegradable physical pollutants, such as plastic, metal, and glass objects in garbage. Chemicals are sometimes dumped in drums, which often leak, allowing their contents to reach the groundwater (water in the rock layers under the ground).

Polluting the Air

The substances that pollute the earth's atmosphere are gases, tiny particles of solids (such as those in smoke), and tiny particles of liquids (vapors). The main atmospheric pollutants are the gas carbon monoxide, gases containing sulfur and nitrogen, and tiny particles of dust and ash from fires. They create smog, which makes breathing difficult and may cause acid rain and global warming. Most of these pollutants come from the burning of fossil fuels (coal, oil, and gas) in engines and power plants.

In rain forest areas, most atmospheric pollution comes from the fires started by slash-and-burn farmers and ranchers. These fires create smoke and large amounts of carbon monoxide and carbon dioxide. Carbon dioxide is a major greenhouse gas that is believed to cause global warming. Large cities close to rain forests suffer from smog caused by smoke from hundreds of forest fires. A series of huge forest fires in Indonesia in 1998 created serious smog in cities such as Jakarta, the capital city. Smoke from the fires could be seen from outer space.

Polluting the Water

Water pollution affects streams, rivers, lakes, seas, and oceans, as well as groundwater. Sewage plus chemicals from factories and farming all cause water pollution. In addition, chemicals accidentally spill from their containers or from factories. Oil slicks from oil tankers that run aground may cause large-scale damage to the environment.

Pollutants in the water poison plants and animals and upset the balance of the food chain. In certain Paraguayan rivers,

Accidental spills of crude oil, such as this one in Nigeria, kill plants and animals. The spills often come from poorly maintained pipelines that carry oil from oil wells to refineries.

A miner panning for gold on the Bulolo River, Papua New Guinea. Mercury, used to purify the gold after it has been extracted, pollutes these rivers.

people are often attacked by piranhas. Normally piranhas attack only wounded or dead animals. However, it was found that the rivers contained waste from cattle farms and slaughterhouses which incited the piranhas to attack healthy people. In nearby rivers with no such contamination, people could swim safely.

In rain forests the main water pollutants are chemicals from spills during mining operations, oil exploration, and logging mills and untreated sewage from shantytowns built to house miners. These pollutants affect life everywhere downstream of where they are dumped. In Colombia, chemical pollutants such as kerosene and sulfuric acid are released from illegal drug-processing plants deep in the rain forest.

IN FOCUS

Precious and Poisonous

In the Amazon River basin, thousands of small teams of gold miners work along riverbanks. They wash silt into pans to find tiny particles of gold. Then they use mercury, which is a silvery, liquid metal, to help separate the gold from the silt. The mercury spills into rivers and escapes into the air as a vapor. Mercury is extremely poisonous and damages nerves and brain tissue. It gets into the food chain through microscopic river creatures and is then taken in by fish and eventually humans. Mercury poisoning is likely to create major health problems for Brazilians in the future.

Reducing Pollution

It is easy to see the effects of pollution on the earth and its plants and animals, but it is more difficult to reduce the amount of pollution we put into the environment. Reducing pollution normally costs time and money. For example, expensive machinery must be installed at power plants to remove pollutants from the plants' exhaust gases. Rain forest countries lack the funds for this kind of high-tech investment. For individual miners living and working in poor conditions in the rain forest, there is little incentive to worry about the pollution they create.

Check these out:

Carbon Cycle • **Dolphin** • **Exploitation** • **Global Warming** • **Human Interference** • **Mining** • **Oil Exploration**

Possum

Possums and opossums are marsupials related to kangaroos. A marsupial is a mammal, but unlike other mammals, the mother usually carries her offspring in a pouch on her belly. The baby is born tiny and helpless and feeds from milk produced from nipples in the mother's pouch. The pouch protects it until it is large enough to fend for itself.

KEY FACTS

- **Both possums and opossums are mainly nocturnal, spending the day asleep, often in a leaf nest high up in a tree.**
- **Possums and opossums vary in size from that of a mouse to that of a small domestic cat.**

Possums

Possums, also commonly called phalangers, all come from Australia and New Guinea. They have the widest distribution of all of the marsupial families, and not all of them dwell in the rain forest. The koala bear, for example, is a possum, but it lives in dry gum forests. Possums eat a range of foods including flowers, pollen, fruit, leaves, insects, larvae, and even small birds.

Possums vary in size and overall shape, but they share the habit of living in trees. Some have large ears, while others have small ears hidden by thick fur. Nearly all of them have long tails, which are usually covered in fur for about the first half and then naked for the rest. In some species, however, the tail is completely covered in fur. At the small end of the scale, the pygmy possum from New Guinea resembles a dormouse in appearance and is just 3 to 4 inches (7 to 11 cm) long with a tail up to 7 inches (17 cm)

The spotted cuscus is a possum that lives in the rain forests of Papua New Guinea and Australia.

long. The larger possums include the rare spotted cuscus of northern Australia and Papua New Guinea, which has a body length of 14 to 18 inches (35 to 45 cm), and the brush-tipped ring-tailed possum, which comes only from the Queensland rain forest and looks like a lemur.

IN FOCUS

Flying Possums

A number of possums can glide through the air from tree to tree. Like the flying squirrels of the North American forests, these possums have broad flaps of skin along the sides of the body, running from the front to the hind legs. These flaps form a gliding surface when the legs are held outstretched. The gliding possum from New Guinea can glide for up to 20 ft. (6 m) and has been seen to catch moths in midair. It feeds on insects, small birds, nectar, sap, flowers, and buds. An even larger gliding possum (below) from the Queensland rain forest of Australia can glide as far as 30 ft. (9 m).

Opossums

Opossums are related to possums but are found only in the Americas. Though they are marsupials, not all species have pouches. There are around 70 species altogether, with 50 or so species living in the rain forests. Like the possums, they vary greatly in size and shape. The smallest and the larger opossums have a long prehensile tail, which can be coiled around twigs and branches to support the animal like an extra arm. Short-tailed opossums have long, thin snouts and look like shrews. In general they eat the same sorts of food as the possums—insects and spiders, other small animals, fruit, and nectar.

Two more unusual species are the water opossum and the lutrine opossum. Good swimmers, water opossums have webbed hind feet. They catch fish, crayfish, and other water creatures from forest streams and rivers, but they also hunt for small prey away from water. The female has a special pouch that seals up to prevent water from entering when she is swimming. The lutrine opossum resembles a weasel or small otter and hunts small animals.

Check these out:

Feeding • Locomotion • Mammal • Nocturnal Animal • Tree Kangaroo

Primate

Primates are the group of mammals that includes monkeys, apes, and humans. They are divided into two main groupings. The first kind, the prosimians, includes the most primitive of the primates. These still retain the rather protruding snout more typical of other mammals, such as dogs and civets. Prosimians also retain the moist nose that gives them a keen sense of smell. Prosimians such as the lemurs (LEE-muhrs) from Madagascar depend upon their sense of smell, and many species mark trees in their territories with scent from special glands. Other prosimians are lorises, pottos, and galagos (guh-LAE-goes). Lorises are found from tropical Africa to Asia, but pottos and galagos are confined to Africa.

KEY FACTS

- **There are about 177 species of primates on Earth; many of these are now endangered.**
- **The rufous mouse lemur weighs about the same as a slice of white bread.**
- **Tarsier mothers carry their small babies in their mouths.**
- **The night or owl monkey is the only nocturnal primate from the Americas.**

The prominent doglike snout and moist nose of this blue–eyed lemur are typical of prosimians. This lemur is feeding on a hibiscus flower.

The second main primate group is the simians, which are more physically advanced than the prosimians and of higher intelligence. The simians include monkeys of the Americas (including marmosets and tamarins), monkeys of Africa and Asia (including baboons), apes (including chimpanzees), and humans. For most of these primates, sight and sound are more important than their sense of smell.

One primate that fails to fit neatly into any of these groups is the tarsier, which shares characteristics with both groups. Three tarsier species occur in the rain forests of Southeast Asia. Tarsiers are some of the smallest primates, and, as with many nocturnal creatures, they have huge eyes.

IN FOCUS

Rufous Mouse Lemur

The rufous mouse lemur is one of the world's smallest primates; it weighs just 1.5 to 3 oz. (42 to 85 g). It is restricted to the rain forests in the eastern part of Madagascar. Unlike many of the larger lemurs, it is not imminently threatened with extinction, since it is widespread and can survive in very disturbed forests. Like the almost equally small tarsier, it lives in the forest understory among the tangle of vines and lianas, jumping nimbly around in its nocturnal hunt for insects and fruit. During the day several individuals come together to sleep in a nest of leaves or in a tree hole.

The common squirrel monkey is the smallest of the true South American monkeys. It lives in large groups within the rain forest.

A gibbon and her baby. Gibbons are long-armed apes that live almost exclusively in the trees.

A Rain Forest Home

Rain forest is by far the most important habitat for primates, and primates are by far the most abundant and conspicuous mammals in many rain forests. Africa, Asia, and tropical America each have about 45 species of rain forest primates, while Madagascar has about 15. The densest primate populations occur in the rain forests of central Africa. The highest species counts—of up to 14 species—come from specific sites in Amazonia and central Africa. Madagascar's best locality has 12 species, while in Asia only 7 species may be found in the richest sites in West Malaysia and Sumatra.

Gripping Hands

Most primates have very nimble fingers that can grip objects firmly because of their opposable thumbs. These can be moved so as to work in consort with the fingers, permitting quite a fine degree of control over what is being held. Unlike humans, all other primates also have opposable big toes. Some primates, such as gibbons and spider monkeys, have a long, flexible tail that acts as a fifth hand. The tail's prehensile tip enables it to curl around and grasp branches so firmly that the animal can hang quite safely, suspended solely from its tail.

Check these out:

Africa · **Ape** · **Chimpanzee** · **Galago** · **Gibbon** · **Gorilla** · **Lemur** · **Locomotion** · **Loris** · **Mammal** · **Marmoset and Tamarin** · **Monkey** · **Orangutan**

Quinault People

The Quinault (kwin-OLT) are a native people of North America's temperate rain forest. They are located on the central Pacific Coast of Washington State.

Most Quinaults live in the coastal towns of Taholah and Queets on and near the Quinault Reservation. The reservation was established by treaty with the United States in 1855. It consists of over 200,000 acres (84,000 ha) and extends from the coast to the Olympic Mountains in the east. Today there are about 2,500 Quinault people.

KEY FACTS

- **Timber companies are destroying the fish habitat in the streams upon which the Quinault depend.**
- **Today there are about 2,500 Quinault people.**

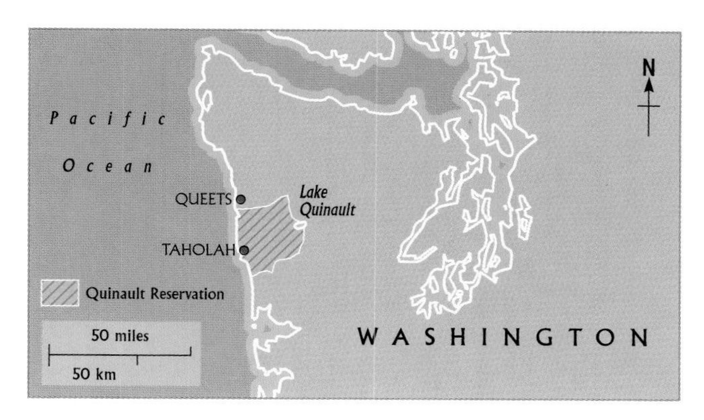

Rain Forest Products

Historically, the Quinault land was so abundant in natural resources, especially salmon, that the people did not have to struggle for survival. They had leisure time for storytelling and great feasts called potlatches, where the hosts would give away many of their possessions to their guests.

The temperate rain forest provided the Quinaults with their building materials. The cedar tree was probably the most important. Quinault villages consisted of large cedar buildings that housed a number of families. The buildings had a gabled roof and were long rectangles, about twice as long as the width of the building. They were built along the banks of the salmon streams, laid out east to west, with the door facing east.

The rain forest also provided the women with cedar bark, which was their most important material for making clothing. The women were skilled at

A stream in the Quinault rain forest. The rain forest is home to many plant varieties. Down through the centuries Quinault medical practitioners have learned medicinal uses for many of the plants.

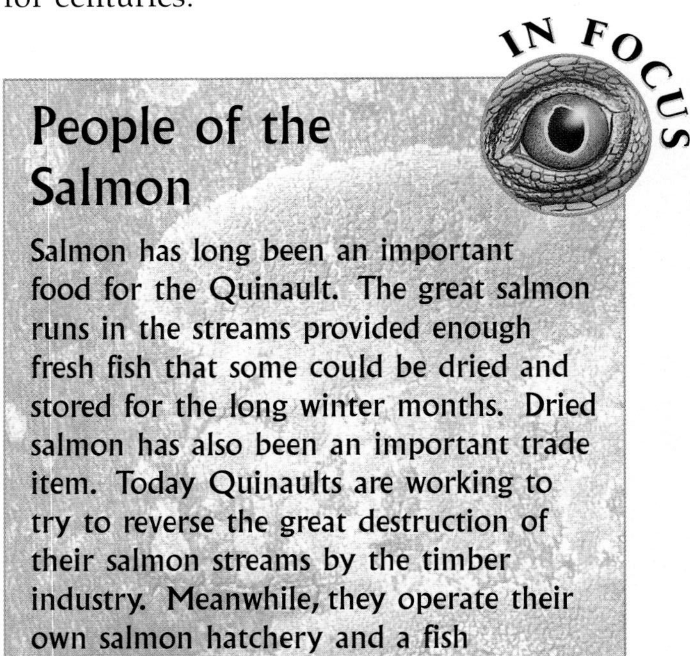

Quinault Indian Skeeter Underwood fishing for blueback (Chinook) salmon along Washington's Quinault River.

fashioning the cedar bark into skirts. They could also weave it into mats. For protection from the excessive rain, waterproof cattail was used to make hats and raincoats.

Cultural Life

The rain forest is still an essential part of the Quinaults' cultural life. Every Quinault young man ventures deep into the rain forest to experience a vision quest. During this important ceremony, the young man receives a spirit protector.

Young women do not go on vision quests into the forest. Instead they observe rituals involved with coming-of-age for marriage. A young woman remains in isolation for five months at that time.

The Quinaults have been known for mostly peaceful relations with neighboring groups. They have carried on a wide trade with other peoples up and down the coast.

Defending Rights

The tribal government has worked hard to fight the destruction of Quinault land. Most of their forest has been clear-cut, and the timber companies replanted only one percent of that land. The erosion from the heavy rains polluted the streams and ruined the salmon fishing. In 1989 the Quinaults were awarded $26 million in compensation for some of that damage.

The state of Washington wanted to build a highway through their land that would lead to easier access and further destruction, but the Quinaults were able to prevent the road from being built. They also closed miles of their beaches to prevent further harm to them by careless tourists.

Today most Quinaults still live in their native homeland. They are trying to restore it to the place of great natural abundance that they had known for centuries.

IN FOCUS

People of the Salmon

Salmon has long been an important food for the Quinault. The great salmon runs in the streams provided enough fresh fish that some could be dried and stored for the long winter months. Dried salmon has also been an important trade item. Today Quinaults are working to try to reverse the great destruction of their salmon streams by the timber industry. Meanwhile, they operate their own salmon hatchery and a fish processing plant.

Check these out:

North America • **People of the Rain Forest** • **Temperate Rain Forest**

Rafflesia

Rafflesias (ruh-FLEE-zee-uhs) are among the world's strangest plants. They produce enormous flowers, yet they have no roots, stems, or leaves. They are parasites, getting all their food from the lianas (lee-AH-nuhs) on which they grow.

Most of the rafflesia plant consists of hairlike threads growing inside the roots and the lower parts of the stems of the lianas. The threads soak up food from the lianas, and they soon start to produce their flowers.

Orange buds as big as cabbages burst through the bark of the lianas and gradually open to form five thick petals, like big pieces of orange peel. A large hollow in the middle of the male flower contains pollen-producing stamens or seed-producing carpels in the case of female flowers. The flower smells like rotting meat, and this attracts the flies that will help pollinate it. The flies swarm all over the inside of the flower, and if it is a male flower, they get dusted with pollen from the stamens. When the flies visit a female flower, some of this pollen finds its way to the carpels. This process is called pollination, and it triggers the formation of fruits and seeds.

The fruits have a creamy flesh that contain thousands of very small seeds.

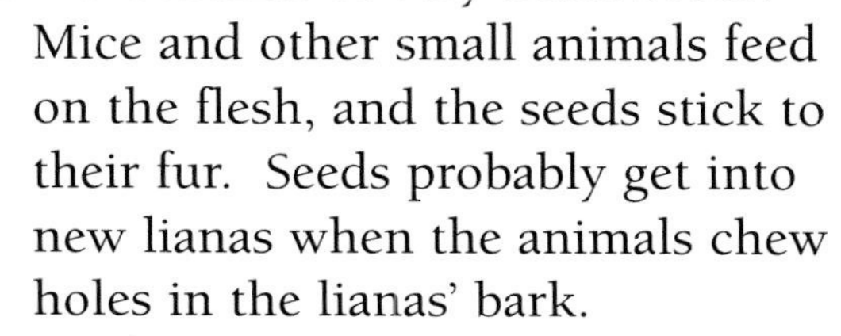

Mice and other small animals feed on the flesh, and the seeds stick to their fur. Seeds probably get into new lianas when the animals chew holes in the lianas' bark.

About a dozen kinds of rafflesia live in the forests of Malaysia and Indonesia. *Rafflesia arnoldii* produces the world's biggest individual flower. It is up to 3 feet (1 m) across and weighs about 20 pounds (9 kg). This plant grows only on the islands of Borneo and Sumatra, and it is an endangered species. It does not flower very often, and there is always great excitement among locals and scientists when the flower appears.

Rafflesia arnoldii *is the world's largest individual flower: it can be as much as 3 ft. (1 m) across. It attracts flies with its smell of rotting meat.*

Check these out:

Flowering Plant **Parasite** **Plant** **Pollination**

Rain Forest

Rain forests occur in places where rain falls more or less throughout the year, without a prolonged dry period. Even when some months are drier than others, the driest months usually have at least some rainfall, so there is never a state of real drought.

KEY FACTS

- **New Zealand's black tree fern is the world's tallest tree fern.**
- **Some tropical rain forest trees are more than 2,000 years old.**
- **Even today, many tropical rain forest areas have not been fully explored on foot.**

Rain Forest Structure

At first glance, a rain forest seems to be a mass of trees with no sign of any particular pattern or structure. In reality, the rain forest is much more organized than it at first appears. If you cut a vertical section through the forest, a number of distinct layers emerge, though not all will be found in every type of rain forest.

Looking down on the forest from above, the tops of the largest trees form the forest canopy layer. Some giant tree species grow so large that they reach above the canopy here and there as emergent layer species. Below the canopy but not easily visible from above is the subcanopy layer, made up of smaller trees reaching up to but not as high as the canopy. Below the subcanopy are bushes and smaller trees, which form the understory. Finally, down in the gloomy depths of the forest floor, there is a ground layer of non-woody herbs, including flowering plants such as gingers and hot-lips.

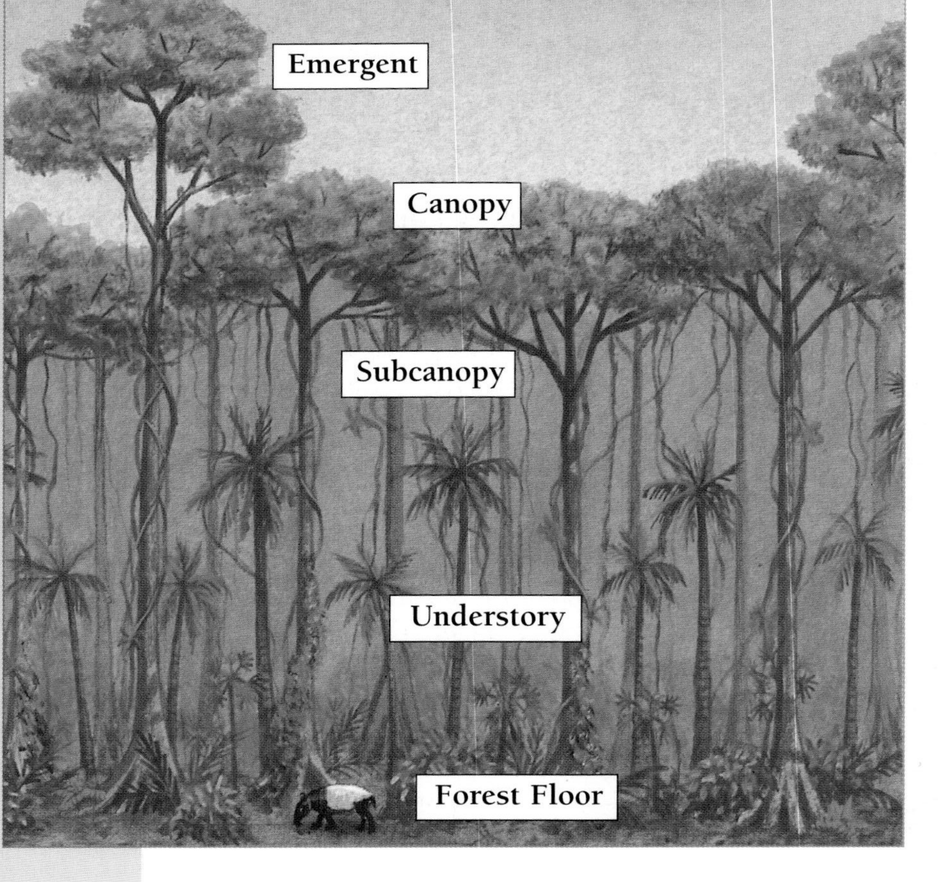

There are several different types of rain forests. Whether or not an area is covered by rain forest of one kind or another is dictated by the level of rainfall. Whether or not a forest is tropical, subtropical, or temperate is dictated by temperature and latitude. Tropical plants are unable to tolerate frost and will therefore never be found in an area where the temperature may, even if only rarely, fall below freezing. Where the temperatures can fall below freezing, the rain forest is temperate.

The high rainfall in the temperate Hoh Rain Forest in Washington State promotes a dense growth of ferns in the permanently saturated air.

Temperate Rain Forest

Temperate rain forests are established in quite limited areas. The special climatic and geographic conditions needed for their development are found only in places along the west coast of North America, in southern Chile and Argentina, and in Japan, Tasmania, and New Zealand. In all these areas, winters are relatively mild because the forests are located between mountains on one side and the sea on the other. This also gives rise to abundant rainfall throughout the year, reaching almost 160 inches (4,000 mm) in some North American forests. Frequent dense enshrouding fogs also help keep these forests permanently dripping with moisture.

Subtropical Rain Forest

Subtropical rain forests occur only where special protective environmental conditions allow the growth of rain forest. High rainfall and relative protection from frost are important factors, although light frosts do occur on some nights of the year. However, in some years devastating and prolonged frosts may suddenly strike and damage the plant and animal life, as happened in South America in July 1975. This seems to be a limiting factor in biodiversity, which is always lower than in true tropical rain forests. Subtropical rain forests occur in South America, southern Madagascar, parts of Asia (such as southern China), and Australia.

Tropical Rain Forest

Tropical rain forest is by far the most important type of rain forest, both because of the relatively huge area it covers compared to the other types, and because of the vast range of plants and animals that are found nowhere else in the world. Tropical rain forests are concentrated in a belt around the equator, where the climate is constantly both warm and wet. Unlike places farther north or south, really high temperatures are absent. It is the constancy of the warmth that is important, not its maximum values which never approach those on a really hot summer's day in New York City or Chicago, for

IN FOCUS

New Zealand's Trees

The rain forests of New Zealand may be saturated with 10 in. (25 cm) of rain during any 24-hour period. The trees there include rimu, tawa, matai (black pine, which grows to 100 ft. or 30 m), rata, and various kinds of southern beeches. The rimu or red pine can reach a height of 165 ft. (50 m) and has high-quality timber, while the rata is noted for its mass of crimson blossoms. Like the strangler figs of the tropical rain forests, the rata starts out as an epiphyte: it sends roots down to the ground and eventually stifles its host tree. Huge tree ferns often form dense groves; the mamaku or black tree fern can reach 66 ft. (20 m).

example. Of course, on the other hand, temperatures in tropical rain forests never fall much below a level regarded as "pleasant," and never plummet to the subzero temperatures found over much of North America during wintertime.

The rain forests' regular water supplies are also dependent on the constant heat. Heat causes the moisture-laden trade winds converging on the tropical belt to rise, generating rainfall as the air cools and can no longer hang on to its heavy load of moisture.

Over half the world's tropical rain forests are in Central and South America, mostly in Amazonia, which contains the biggest forest on Earth. Southeast Asia has the next largest area of rain forest, followed by Africa, Australia and New Guinea, and islands such as Madagascar.

Life-Support Systems

Tropical rain forests once covered about one seventh of the world's land surface, but they have been reduced by about half over the last 100 years. The millions of trees in these forests help purge the air of pollutants caused by human activities. They also help to regulate the world's weather and generate vast amounts of rainfall. A single huge rain forest tree acts like a giant pump, discharging 200 gallons (760 liters) of water into the atmosphere every day of the year. This means that any given area of rain forest contributes 20 times as much to cloud formation as the equivalent area of the sea's surface. Rain forest trees also lock up huge amounts of carbon dioxide, which is released in vast quantities by automobiles and the burning of coal and other fossil fuels, causing the current global warming crisis. Tropical rain forests are estimated to hold some 90 percent of all the plant and animal species on Earth, many of which could be of potential benefit to humanity in medicine and other areas.

One striking aspect of the tropical rain forest is the huge variety of trees compared with a temperate forest. One tract of Amazonian forest in Peru has more than 120 species of trees per acre (300 per hectare), compared with perhaps 30 to 40 per acre (75 to 100 per hectare) in some of the richest North American forests. Another characteristic of many rain forests is the abundance of epiphytic plants (although these are not noticeably abundant in Amazonia). Some trees may be burdened with a mass of epiphytes weighing one third as much as the tree.

A dense growth of palms is one of the characteristics of the understory of most of the world's tropical rain forests, as here in Guyana.

Lowland Tropical Rain Forest

Forest type varies according to altitude. Lowland tropical rain forest is usually characterized by the tallest trees and the highest plant and animal diversity. The canopy in Malaysian forests often reaches a height of 200 to 230 feet (60 to 70 m). Most of the forest's activities go on out of sight of the ground up in the treetops, because that is where sunlight is most abundant. The sun is the energy source that powers the trees' production of the leaves, flowers, and fruits that provide the basis for most of the forest's food chains. The canopy is so productive of food that a whole range of animals have evolved to live and feed there, including monkeys, marmosets, porcupines, sloths, anteaters, opossums, kinkajous, and rats, plus frogs, snakes, lizards, a huge range of birds, and countless insects.

Forests at High Altitudes

Lowland forest gradually changes to lower montane forest somewhere around 5,000 feet (1,500 m), with a slightly lower canopy and an increase in ferns and mosses. Above about 10,000 feet (3,000 m) there is a change to cloud forest, a weird realm of constant twilight as dense clouds hang almost permanently over the dripping wet trees. The trees' rather short trunks are

IN FOCUS

Monteverde Cloud Forest

The reserve at Monteverde in the Cordillera de Tilarán in Costa Rica is the most visited cloud forest in the world. Visitor pressure is so great that the authorities have been obliged to pave the most frequently used paths through the forests to avoid further wear and tear on the fragile environment. The forest contains more than 2,000 species of plants and some 320 kinds of birds. The quarry that most bird enthusiasts come to track down, the resplendent quetzal (ket-SAHL), is common and easy to observe. However, the 100 different kinds of mammals, including jaguars and ocelots, are seldom spotted. Several more reserves have recently been purchased alongside Monteverde, conserving a higher proportion of the precious remaining cloud forest, with its vital function not only of preserving nature but of protecting the invaluable watershed.

gnarled and twisted, while every limb is garlanded with thick mats of mosses, lichens, ferns, bromeliads, orchids (up to 50 different species on a single tree), and other epiphytic plants. It is a startling fact that in cloud forests nearly half the total weight of all the living organisms (biomass) can be epiphytes. Generally these rather cool and dank places are less rich in animal species than lowland forests, though hummingbirds are far more abundant and diverse in cloud forests than in the lowland Amazonian forests.

Above the cloud forest lies another zone in which the trees are even more stunted and twisted, often being little more than head-high. This is called elfin forest, and even the mosses and other epiphytes of the cloud forest are often absent, replaced by thick mats of tough lichens. Trees no larger than three feet (1 m) tall may be hundreds of years old, because the low light levels and constant cold retard growth. Even up here there are special animals, such as the spectacled bear of the Andean elfin forests. As with the lowland rain forests, even these montane forests have been greatly reduced for agriculture and firewood.

Check these out:

Climate and Weather • Evolution of the Rain Forest • Monsoon Rain Forest • Subtropical Rain Forest • Temperate Rain Forest • Tropical Rain Forest

Rattan

Rattans belong to the palm family, but they are very unusual palms. They are climbing plants, and instead of the stout, straight stems of most palms, they have weak, ropelike stems. With lengths often in excess of 600 feet (180 m), these are by far the world's longest stems, although they are rarely much thicker than a person's finger. The thickest ones are only about 4 inches (10 cm) in diameter.

KEY FACTS

- **The longest rattan stem on record was about 790 ft. (240 m) long.**
- **Rattan stems are often so dense that they bind the treetops together, and they can even hold up large trees after the trunks have been cut through.**
- **The large bud at the tip of each rattan stem is very nutritious. When animals eat these buds, stems are prevented from growing any further, but new shoots quickly sprout from the base.**

Rattans climb by means of sharp, curved spines scattered over the stems and undersides of their leaves and on whiplike outgrowths. These spines latch on to neighboring plants like grappling hooks and hold the rattans in place. The plants may grow as much as 30 feet (9 m) per year as they strive to reach the forest canopy and spread their leafy crowns. They are often so abundant that their combined weight is enough to bring trees crashing down, but this is not the end of the rattans. They continue to grow, twisting over the ground and forming impenetrable thickets like coils of barbed wire until they find new trees to climb.

Having reached the forest canopy, the rattans produce huge bunches of small flowers, which are pollinated mainly by bees. They then bear colorful, fleshy, and often very tasty fruits. Birds, monkeys, and fruit bats feed on the fruits and scatter the seeds. The sun bear of Southeast Asia is also very fond of rattan fruits.

A Useful Plant

Climbing palms grow in all rain forest areas, but the true rattans occur only in Southeast Asia and, to a lesser extent, in Africa. There are nearly 600 different kinds. About 20 of them are commercially important, providing some of

This piece of rattan stem shows the wicked spines with which the rattans cling to the supporting trees. Removing the spines from the plant is difficult and can be painful.

Southeast Asia's most valuable exports. Thousands of tons are harvested every year for making cane furniture, and thousands of people earn a living from harvesting and preparing the cane. The larger stems are used for the legs of chairs and sofas, while the thinner ones are split lengthwise to provide the flexible cane used for the seats. Many walking sticks and umbrella handles are also made from rattans, mostly from a species commonly known as Malacca cane. There are probably few homes anywhere in the developed world that do not contain at least one item manufactured from rattan.

Rattans are also of great importance in the lives of the indigenous forest people of Southeast Asia. The few remaining nomadic Penan (PEH-nahn) people of Borneo make temporary shelters by lashing poles together with rattans, and they also make all their food-gathering baskets and baby carriers from the split stems. Good drinking water can also be obtained from fresh rattan stems by cutting them open.

These rattan collectors have had a successful day in the Indonesian rain forest. Each is carrying a coiled stem from which all the leaves and thorns have been stripped.

The more settled agricultural people of the region use rattan in their longhouses. These big houses, often raised on stilts, are built by lashing large poles or tree trunks together with rattans. They accommodate dozens of families, each with its own living area separated from neighboring families by partitions. The partitions are made by binding the split rattan stems into large sheets. Carpets and even roof panels are made in the same way.

IN FOCUS

Rattans and Ants

Korthalsia rattans regularly shelter colonies of ants. The insects make their homes in little pockets that develop where the leaf bases join the stems. The pockets remain even when the old leaf blades have fallen, and a large stem may have hundreds of such pockets. In return for their lodgings, the ants protect the rattans from leaf-eating insects. If the plant is disturbed by a larger animal, the ants all tap their jaws on the dry walls of their pockets and produce an eerie rustling sound. If the disturbance continues, they rush out and attack the intruder with their powerful jaws.

Check these out:

Climber ● Exploitation ● Palm Tree

Red Panda

The red panda is a true panda—a relative of the giant panda—but it looks quite different. It is only 20–26 inches (50–65 cm) long and is shaped like an overweight cat with a long tail. It is reddish brown, with black underparts and a white face with a reddish stripe from each eye to the corners of its mouth. Like some cats, it has a faintly striped tail.

The red panda lives in the mountain forests of northeast India, Bhutan, Nepal, and southwest China. Only a few of these forests—the tropical monsoon forests or bamboo forests—can be considered rain forests. The panda has soft thick fur and tends to avoid the heat. The soles of its feet are hairy, which improves its grip on wet branches in the misty mountain forests and on ice-covered rocks at higher altitudes.

A shy animal that lives alone and comes out only at night, the red panda is seldom seen. However, it has a range of calls that carry through the night air. The young will call for their mother with high-pitched whistles. By day it sleeps curled up in a fork or a hollow of a tree, with its tail over its face.

Feeding

The red panda feeds mainly on plants, including bamboo, fruits, nuts, roots, and lichens (LIE-kuhns), and sometimes also on mice, young birds, eggs, and insects. When feeding, it sits up on its haunches and holds the food in its front paws. It will dip its paw into the soft pulp inside fruits, then lick off the juices. It washes itself like a cat, licking its front paws and wiping them across its forehead and ears.

Family Life

Red pandas usually live alone or in pairs. Males have scent glands on their rumps and mark rocks, logs, and tree stumps in their territory. One to four young are born at a time. They stay with their mothers until they are about five months old, and they can breed at 18 months.

The red panda is equally at home in trees or on the ground. Despite its foxlike appearance, it feeds mainly on plants.

Check these out:

Mammal **Monsoon Rain Forest**

Glossary

Bacteria: a large group of microscopic organisms, found almost everywhere on Earth. Many of them cause diseases and are known as germs.

Canines: the long, sharp, pointed teeth just behind the front teeth of mammals. They are used to pierce and grip prey.

Canopy: the "roof" of the forest, composed of the interlocking branches of the trees that cut off most of the light from the forest floor.

Carpel: the female part of a flower that gives rise to the fruit and seeds after pollination.

Cellulose: an elastic, porous material that is the main component of plant cell walls.

Chlorophyll: the green coloring matter of plants.

Confiscation: taking something away as a punishment for breaking the law.

Decimate: to destroy most of something.

Endemic: a living organism that comes from just one or a few particular areas of the world and is not naturally found anywhere else.

Epiphyte: a name given to any plant that grows on another without taking any food from it. Most epiphytes grow on trees and include many ferns and orchids.

Floodplain: a plain along a river, formed from sediment left there when the river floods.

Global warming: the gradual warming up of the earth's atmosphere, believed to be due to increasing amounts of carbon dioxide in the air.

Hierarchy: the system of ranking in communities of animals or birds, in which each animal knows its own status in relation to the others.

Hunter-gatherer: someone who lives by hunting animals and gathering fruits and roots to eat.

Indigenous: historically native to a particular area.

Liana: common name for any woody climbing plant.

Malaria: a human disease, sometimes fatal, caused by a single-celled animal living in the red blood cells.

Mangrove: a small evergreen tree with tangled, basketlike roots that grows in muddy tidal waters around tropical coasts. There are many different species.

Molecule: the smallest particle of an element or compound, and made up of atoms.

Monsoon forest: certain forests in Asia that have a long dry season and then a long spell of heavy rain.

Nectar: a sweet, sugar-rich, scented liquid produced by flowers to attract animals for pollination.

Nomadic: continually wandering from place to place, with no settled home.

Organism: any living creature, including both animals and plants.

Parasite: a plant or animal that lives on or in another plant or animal and lives at its expense.

Photosynthesis: the process by which green plants use sunlight to combine water, minerals from the soil, and carbon dioxide from the air to make simple sugars, which they use as food.

Pollen: the dustlike material produced by flowers. When carried to another flower by animals or the wind, it triggers the formation of seeds.

Pollination: the transfer of pollen from the stamens to the stigmas of flowers.

Protozoan: common name for any microscopic, single-celled animal.

Spore: a (usually microscopic) structure produced during reproduction to disperse an organism's sex cells. The simplest spore is a single cell with a tough protective coat. Pollen grains are spores that carry the male sex cells from one flower to another.

Stamen: the male part of a flower, where pollen is produced.

Staple food: the main food of a population, which is eaten virtually every day. It is usually rich in starch and it provides the people with most of their energy.

Stigma: the part of the carpel (the female part of the flower) that receives pollen grains during pollination. A flower with a single carpel has a single stigma; a flower with several carpels will have a stigma on each one.

Trade wind: a wind that blows toward the equator from the northeast and southeast. It is caused by hot air rising at the equator.

Understory: the layer of vegetation below the rain forest canopy.

Watershed: an area from which rain is drained away by a particular set of streams and rivers.

Index

All numbers in *italics* indicate photographs.